TRUE
to HIS
WORD

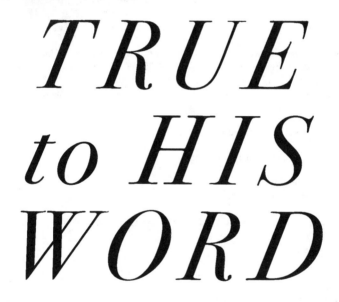

TRUE
to HIS
WORD

100 MEDITATIONS ON THE
FAITHFULNESS OF GOD

JON BLOOM

MOODY PUBLISHERS
CHICAGO

Edited by Pamela Joy Pugh
Interior design: Puckett Smartt
Cover design: Erik M. Peterson
Cover illustration of mountains © 2022 by baoyan / Shutterstock (411631474). All rights reserved.
Author photo: Ryan Stadler

ISBN: 978-0-8024-2829-5

Originally delivered by fleets of horse-drawn wagons, the affordable paperbacks from D. L. Moody's publishing house resourced the church and served everyday people. Now, after more than 125 years of publishing and ministry, Moody Publishers' mission remains the same— even if our delivery systems have changed a bit. For more information on other books (and resources) created from a biblical perspective, go to www.moodypublishers.com or write to

Moody Publishers
820 N. LaSalle Boulevard
Chicago, IL 60610

1 3 5 7 9 10 8 6 4 2

Printed in the United States of America

To Jim
My beloved older brother
and father in Christ Jesus through the gospel,
who, for nearly five decades, has modeled for me
what a "faithful minister and fellow servant in the Lord" looks like.
Colossians 4:7

Contents

Introduction

One hundred meditations on the faithfulness of God. Are there really that many distinct, fresh, soul-nourishing things to say about this divine attribute? That's something I wondered when my friend Trillia Newbell first invited me to tackle this project. But it didn't take long to realize that one hundred meditations would barely scratch the surface of what the Bible has to say about God's faithfulness.

As you make your way through these meditations, you may be surprised at how few of the Scripture texts I've chosen to orient on or exposit contain some form of the word "faithful." There's a reason for this. Most of the texts in Scripture that explicitly mention God's faithfulness are declarations that God possesses this attribute: "The LORD, the LORD, a God merciful and gracious, slow to anger, and abounding in steadfast love and faithfulness" (Ex. 34:6); or they are exclamations in praise of this attribute: "Great is your faithfulness" (Lam. 3:23). But for the most part, they don't include definitions or illustrations of God's faithfulness.

You don't really need it defined anyway. God's faithfulness is a pretty straightforward concept. I state it in the four words that became this book's title, and I only devote one chapter, the first, to explaining what it means.

But you do need illustrations. Because while the concept of God's faithfulness may be straightforward and clear, the ways God chooses to be true to his word frequently are not. So, you need examples of what God's faithfulness looks like in real life, how it manifests in the complex life of faith you experience. And such examples fill the pages of the Bible from beginning to end. God's faithfulness can be seen in every story of redemptive history, every promise, commandment, prophecy, parable, every sign and wonder, teaching, exhortation, every mercy God extends to sinful people, and every judgment he brings upon sinful people.

That's why I say this book barely scratches the surface of this topic. But my hope is that these meditations will help train your eyes to recognize God's faithfulness in places you may not typically look for it, and in providences, especially confusing, disturbing, and painful ones, that typically might not look like God's faithfulness to you. Because the more adept you become at seeing it, the more you'll realize that you'll never exhaust the ways the Bible can show you that "all the paths of the LORD are steadfast love and faithfulness" (Ps. 25:10).

1

God is faithful, by whom you were called into the fellowship of his Son, Jesus Christ our Lord. 1 CORINTHIANS 1:9

True to His Word

GOD IS FAITHFUL

When you were a kid, and you reneged on some commitment you made to one of your friends, I'll bet you heard this angry protest: "You promised!" Why? Because you hadn't been true to your word.

True to your word. That is a clear, concise, accurate definition of what it means to be a faithful person. If you're faithful, there is consistency between your *words* and your *works*, between what you *believe* and how you *behave*, between what you *promise* and what you *perform*. If someone believes they can trust you and you prove faithful, you will increase their faith in you and strengthen the bond between you. If you prove unfaithful, you will deservedly be on the receiving end of an angry protest from someone who believed they could trust you. And you will damage, perhaps even destroy, a precious relationship.

The Bible defines faithfulness the same way. When Scripture describes a person as "faithful," it's almost never referring to how much faith that person possesses, but to how much faith others can place in that person—how much others can trust him or her to perform what has been promised. A faithful person honors, cherishes, maintains, and guards the faith of those who put their trust in them.

That's exactly what we mean when we say, "God is faithful." As Christians, we're saying that God the Father is "able to do what he [has] promised" (Rom. 4:21), that God the Son, the "Word of God" incarnate, is "Faithful and True" (Rev. 19:11, 13), and that God the Holy Spirit, the "Spirit of truth" (1 John 4:6), will not—because he cannot—lie (Heb. 6:18). We're declaring our belief that God honors, cherishes, maintains, and guards the faith of those who put their trust in him by keeping his promises to them—that he is true to his word.

True to his word. That is a clear, concise, accurate definition of God's faithfulness. And it's all quite simple to say, isn't it? But as the Bible illustrates, God's faithfulness is often not anywhere near so simple to see in our experience of this fallen age.

We live in this dystopic swirl of disappointment, disease, disasters, and disarray, where we're subject to futility, war, deceit, financial crises, suffering, grief, depression, dark nights of the soul, and death, all the while constantly battling the sinful desires of the flesh and the eyes and pride of life dwelling in our members (1 John 2:16). It's not surprising that at any given time, as our perceptions are distorted by our disorienting experiences, it can appear to us as though God is not being true to his word, tempting us to level an angry protest against him.

So, having defined what God's faithfulness means, we're going to briefly meditate on ninety-nine sightings of his faithfulness in Scripture, different and sometimes unexpected ways it manifests, to help correct some of our distortions and increase our faith that God's promises are more trustworthy than our perceptions; that we have good reason to believe that "he who calls [us] is faithful; he will surely do it" (1 Thess. 5:24); that he really is true to his word.

PRAYER

Father, I believe you are faithful; help my unbelief (Mark 9:24)! As I meditate on your word, which reflects all the chaos, calamity, sorrow, and sin in the world, help me see your faithfulness more clearly so I will more deeply trust in you with all my heart and not lean on my own understanding (Prov. 3:5). In Jesus' name, amen.

MEDITATE MORE

Read Romans 4 and ponder: What was it about Abraham's faith in God's faithfulness that God counted as righteousness (vv. 20–23)?

2

Trust in the LORD, and do good; dwell in the land and befriend faithfulness. PSALM 37:3

Begin with What You've Been Given

GOD IS FAITHFUL . . . TO TEACH YOU FAITHFULNESS

A faithful person honors, cherishes, maintains, and guards the faith of those who put their trust in him by keeping his promises to them. God's always like this. You and I, on the other hand . . . well, let's just say this proverb was written about people like us:

> Many a man proclaims his own steadfast love,
>   but a faithful man who can find? (Prov. 20:6)

If we're honest, we'll admit this proverbial shoe has fit at times. If we're rigorously honest, we'll admit this shoe fits more often than we care to admit. The truth hurts.

But God knows us, and when he wounds his children with a truth, his purpose is to heal us (Hos. 6:1) and set us free (John 8:32). Our Father is faithful to keep his promise to conform us to the image of Jesus (Rom. 8:29), the "faithful witness" (Rev. 1:5). And he does this, not by downloading faithfulness into us like a software upgrade, but by "training us . . . to live self-controlled, upright, and godly lives in the present age" (Titus 2:12). Like all training, growing in faithfulness is an arduous process. God teaches us to build our capacity for faithfulness much like we build our capacities for anything: by *exercising* what we want to grow.

We all like the idea of a stronger, slimmer body, or becoming proficient in a skill, or building more effective habits for more sustained productivity. But no transformation happens without starting the painful work of exercising what's weak and staying with it until it grows stronger.

The same is true of faithfulness. We all like the idea of being true to the love we've proclaimed, the commitments we've made, and the responsibilities God has entrusted to us. But if unfaithfulness has become a sinful habit in a certain area, because selfishness has taken root and we lack the fortitude to swear to our own hurt and not change (Ps. 15:4), no transformation will occur without the hard, painful work of *exercising* faithfulness.

The good news is that God has provided us everything we need to start exercising today. We begin with what we've been given. Our training regimen is structured around Psalm 37:3: "Trust in the LORD, and do good; dwell in the land and befriend faithfulness." Today's exercises in *befriending faithfulness* are to do whatever it takes for us to *trust in the Lord* for the grace to diligently *do good* to the people and through the responsibilities he's entrusted to us, in the place (*land*) we find ourselves, with the resources he provides. And to do our "work heartily, as for the Lord and not for men" (Col. 3:23).

God is faithful to teach us faithfulness so that we increasingly—like him—honor, cherish, maintain, and guard the faith of those who put their trust in us by being truer to our word. And he will teach us here, in the "land" where he's placed us. And if we befriend faithfulness here, someday our Master will say to us, "Well done, good and faithful servant. You have been faithful over a little; I will set you over much. Enter into the joy of your master" (Matt. 25:23).

PRAYER

Father, thank you for being faithful to teach me faithfulness. Today, whatever it takes, help me trust you fully and "do good to everyone, and especially to those who are of the household of faith" (Gal. 6:10), where you have placed me and with the resources you provide. In Jesus' name, amen.

MEDITATE MORE

Read Psalm 37, written when David was old (v. 25), and note the various ways he describes the dynamic between our faithfulness and God's.

3

And he believed the Lord, *and he counted it to him as righteousness.*
GENESIS 15:6

Will I Believe God?

GOD IS FAITHFUL . . . TO PUSH YOU INTO DEFINING MOMENTS

If you had been a traveling guest among Abram's nomadic group four thousand years ago, and just happened to observe him the night he stepped outside his tent and gazed into the starry heavens, you wouldn't have guessed it was a defining moment in Abram's life, much less a defining moment in world history. Because what made those minutes of quiet stargazing so astronomically important was that an old man, in the deep recesses of his heart, *believed God.*

God had pushed Abram's faith to the brink. It began when God promised this childless, seventy-five-year-old man, "I will make of you a great nation, and I will bless you . . . and in you all the families of the earth shall be blessed" (Gen. 12:2–3). Abram believed God.

Years went by and God did bless Abram with material prosperity, but not with progeny. However, he reaffirmed his promise (Gen. 13:14–16) and Abram believed.

More years went by. God continued to prosper everything Abram did, except procreate. When God again reaffirmed his promise, but again said nothing about how or when it would be fulfilled, Abram, now in his eighties (and Sarai in her seventies), poured out his anguished perplexity in a desperate prayer: "O Lord God, what will you give me, for I continue childless, and the heir of my house is Eliezer of Damascus?" (Gen. 15:2).

This brings us to that monumental, undramatic night. God told Abram, "Look toward heaven, and number the stars, if you are able to number them. . . . So shall your offspring be" (v. 5). He still didn't tell Abram how or when descendants would come. Once again, he reaffirmed his promise.

But this reaffirmation contained an implied question: "Abram, do you believe me, or your own perceptions?" It was a defining moment.

Aged Abram, with a barren, aged wife and a childless tent, looked into the starry, starry sky and in his heart resolved to trust that though he couldn't see how, "God was able to do what he had promised" (Rom. 4:21). Abram believed God. And God "counted it to him as righteousness" (Gen. 15:6).

God leads many of his children to defining moments when our faith seems pushed to the brink. To observers, it might not show. But inside, everything is on the line for us, all hanging on our answer to a simple, life-defining question: Will I believe God's promise over my perception?

Defining moments are expressions of God's faithfulness to us. God uses them to reveal whether we have justifying faith (the kind he counts as righteousness), to bring needed clarity to our commitment, and to help our unbelief (see Mark 9:24) by forcing us to lay aside the excess weight of nagging doubts (Heb. 12:1).

But our defining moments can also be expressions of God's faithfulness to an untold number of others. For in walking "by faith, not by sight" (2 Cor. 5:7) in this world, we also become channels through which God's saving grace flows to others. These channels of grace connect with others for years, even centuries beyond us, adding more stars to Abram's sky.

PRAYER

Father, thank you for being faithful to me. Whatever it takes, help me walk in a manner worthy of you and fully pleasing to you (Col. 1:10). And since without faith it is impossible to please you (Heb. 11:6), help me lay aside any weight of unbelief and, if necessary, push me into a faith-defining moment. In Jesus' name, amen.

MEDITATE MORE

Paul wrote, "No unbelief made [Abram] waver concerning the promise of God" (Rom. 4:20). Why isn't Abram's perplexed prayer in Genesis 15:2–3 an example of wavering faith?

4

But this I call to mind, and therefore I have hope: The steadfast love of the LORD never ceases; his mercies never come to an end; they are new every morning; great is your faithfulness. LAMENTATIONS 3:21–23

This I Call to Mind

GOD IS FAITHFUL . . . EVEN WHEN YOUR HOPE HAS DIED

This is, arguably, one of the Bible's most beloved declarations of God's love, mercy, and faithfulness. What's surprising is that it comes from what is, arguably, the Bible's saddest book: Lamentations.

The book's author wrote of the nightmarish horrors he'd witnessed as the Babylonian army first laid siege and then laid waste to Jerusalem. He saw priests massacred (Lam. 2:20), women raped, men enslaved (Lam. 5:11–13), young and old slaughtered in the streets (Lam. 2:21; 4:7–8), and starvation-crazed citizens resort to cannibalism (Lam. 4:10). Then, like a spear thrust into Israel's spiritual heart, he saw the Babylonians raze Solomon's great temple to the ground (Lam. 2:6–7).

But the author knew he and his people hadn't been mere victims of ruthless Babylonian imperialism: "The LORD has done what he purposed; he has carried out his word, which he commanded long ago" (Lam. 2:17). After centuries of prophetic warnings, God had finally brought upon his rebellious people (Isa. 1:7–9; Amos 2:4–5) the dreadful covenant curses Moses had pronounced (Deut. 28:47–57).

So the author lamented that God had "driven [him] into darkness without any light," "enveloped [him] with bitterness and tribulation," and "shut out [his] prayer" (Lam. 3:2, 5, 8). No wonder he wrote, "My soul is bereft of peace; I have forgotten what happiness is" and "my endurance has perished; so has my hope from the LORD" (Lam. 3:17–18).

By all appearances, everything was lost. God, in his righteous wrath, administered through a foreign superpower, had slain his "firstborn son" (Ex. 4:22). The tomb had effectively been sealed. All one could do was weep beside the grave—or hide from those with power to kill. Sound familiar?

Suddenly, light shone in the grieving author's darkness: "But this I call to mind, and therefore I have hope" (Lam. 3:21). What did he recall that revived his dead hope? The word of the Lord whose judgment had buried his hope. He recalled that God is "merciful and gracious . . . abounding in steadfast love and faithfulness" (Ex. 34:6), and that God promised to extend his steadfast love and mercy "from everlasting to everlasting" to those who fear him (Ps. 103:17). All was not lost. God would not let his firstborn son remain in the tomb. God's word became a light in his darkness (Ps. 119:105).

This lamenting poet likely didn't realize his words would so powerfully foreshadow Jesus, the Word made flesh (John 1:14), the "light [that] shines in the darkness" (John 1:5), who endured the judgment of destruction we deserved. But reading his poems through New Testament lenses, he reminds us that in our darkest places, when we've "forgotten what happiness is," when it feels like our "endurance has perished" and "so has [our] hope from the LORD" (Lam. 3:17–18), Jesus is the greatest expression of God's unceasing, merciful steadfast love for us. And Jesus, through his Spirit, loves to resurrect our hope by helping us call to mind his "precious and very great promises" (2 Peter 1:4). And when his light shines in our darkness, "the darkness [will] not overcome it" (John 1:5). For great is his faithfulness.

PRAYER

Father, thank you for your unceasing steadfast love, your never-ending mercies, and your great faithfulness. Help me experience them anew today, and should I find my hope perishing, help me call to mind the promises that will revive my hope in you. In Jesus' name, amen.

MEDITATE MORE

Read Psalm 103, then read Lamentations 3:19–33. How many echoes of the psalm do you hear in the lament?

5

For we walk by faith, not by sight. 2 CORINTHIANS 5:7

Fly by the Instruments

GOD IS FAITHFUL . . . TO GUIDE YOU IN SPIRITUAL STORMS

On July 16, 1999, John Kennedy Jr.'s single-engine Piper Saratoga crashed into the Atlantic Ocean off the coast of Martha's Vineyard, killing John, his wife, Carolyn, and Carolyn's sister Lauren. All investigations into the cause pointed to a phenomenon called "spatial disorientation."[1] This occurs when a pilot flies into conditions that prevent him from seeing the horizon or the ground. Reference points that normally guide his senses disappear. His sensory perceptions become unreliable, and he can no longer discern up from down. It can be deadly.

This has a spiritual parallel, one that many saints in Scripture and across the ages (myself included) have experienced when we've "flown" into spiritual storms, with names like "dark nights of the soul" and "faith crises."[2] We lose sight of familiar reference points and become spiritually disoriented. In confused fear, we lurch back and forth trying to regain our bearings, and often begin to spiral down.

Most planes are equipped with navigational instruments. If a pilot enters conditions where his sensory perceptions become unreliable, he can "fly by the instruments." But this is much harder than it sounds.

Under normal conditions, we're usually wise to trust our brain's instinctive instructions to escape danger. But when a pilot is spatially disoriented, his desperately urgent instincts are based on unreliable sensory data. So, if everything in him is shouting "Bank right!" but the instruments indicate he should hold steady, he will instinctively doubt the instruments. As one expert stated, reflecting on the Kennedy crash, "You have to be well trained to disregard what your brain is saying . . . and fly by the instruments."[3] John had not received this training.

This also has a spiritual parallel. In disorienting spiritual storms, we must learn, like pilots, that our subjective perceptions are unreliable. We must train ourselves to place our faith in the objective instruments of God's promises and warnings in Scripture. To paraphrase our text, we must fly by faith, not by sight (2 Cor. 5:7). But this is harder than it sounds.

When our "skies" are clear and our spiritual reference points are in sight, it's easy to imagine confidently relying on the Bible's navigational instruments in some spiritual storm. But, as experienced pilots testify, a real storm is nothing like we imagine. We don't realize how much we rely on our perceptions until we experience the fear of real disorientation and feel the compelling power of our perceptions commanding us to doubt the instruments. We need training.

But faith training isn't like flight training. There aren't faith simulators to prepare us for spiritual storms or human faith instructors to grab the controls if we panic. We must learn by flying in a real storm.

The Holy Spirit is the best instructor. If we listen, he'll faithfully equip us to use the biblical instruments and instruct us through the experience and example of saints whose storms made them skilled at flying by faith, not by sight. And what all these saints (and I with them) testify is that in a spiritual storm, though our disoriented perceptions demand otherwise, we're always wise to fly by the instruments.

PRAYER

Father, thank you for faithfully providing all I need to endure any spiritual storm I may face. Whatever it takes, teach me to "fly by the instruments" so that should I become spiritually disoriented, I will not "lean on [my] own understanding" (Prov. 3:5). In Jesus' name, amen.

MEDITATE MORE

Read through Hebrews 11, identify the spiritual storms each saint endured, and what it meant for them to "fly by the instruments."

6 | *My God, my God, why have you forsaken me? Why are you so far from saving me, from the words of my groaning? O my God, I cry by day, but you do not answer, and by night, but I find no rest.*

PSALM 22:1–2

"I Will Never Forsake You"

GOD IS FAITHFUL . . . EVEN WHEN YOU FEEL FORSAKEN BY HIM

Those anguished opening words of Psalm 22 were penned by King David, who also composed Psalm 23, which opens like this:

> The LORD is my shepherd; I shall not want. He makes me lie down in green pastures. He leads me beside still waters. He restores my soul. He leads me in paths of righteousness for his name's sake. (vv. 1–3)

These two psalms are about as different as they could be. It's almost hard to believe they were written by the same person. In Psalm 22, David feels forsaken by an unresponsive God; in Psalm 23, he feels shepherded by an ever-attentive God. In Psalm 22, David's soul is in restless agony; in Psalm 23, his soul is resting in the care of his Good Shepherd.

I love that these two psalms are back-to-back, because they illustrate how different a saint's experience of God can be. But there's a deeper beauty in this poetic juxtaposition. Both psalms foreshadow and prophesy of Jesus. And in that light, we see that the order in which they appear is no accident.

We know Psalm 22:1, because Jesus screamed it in unfathomable agony on the cross: "Eli, Eli, lema sabachthani?" (Matt. 27:46). *Selah*. At the crux of history, there was a moment when God was God-forsaken.

And he was forsaken for you. And me. The eternal radiance of the Father's glory and "the exact imprint of his nature" (Heb. 1:3) became in that darkest moment *our* unholy sin (2 Cor. 5:21). And for that moment, the holy Father could not abide the holy Son made unholy. God became the object of God's wrath to eternally remove our curse, that we might become the objects of God's eternal mercy, clothed forever with his holiness and righteousness (2 Cor. 5:21).

In Psalm 22, God not only provides us words to pray during our desolate seasons, but he also helps us grasp the desolation Jesus experienced to purchase our peace and restoration.

That is the promise of Psalm 23, purchased by the price of Psalm 22: your Good Shepherd will restore your soul forever. Which makes the order of the psalms fitting. Jesus was forsaken by God, scorned by men, and pierced in his hands and feet (Ps. 22:1, 6–7, 16). For *your* sake. So that he could guide you through every evil valley, honor you before every evil enemy, pursue you with goodness and mercy *every day* of your earthly life—even days you feel forsaken—and bring you to live with him in his house forever (Ps. 23:4–6).

Do you feel forsaken by God? Jesus understands and sympathizes with you—more than you know (Heb. 4:15). Psalm 22 may be your song for brief nights, but Psalm 23 will be your song for an eternal morning (Ps. 30:5). And for all your lonely nights or refreshing mornings he makes this promise of faithfulness: "I will never leave you nor forsake you" (Heb. 13:5).

PRAYER

Father, thank you for the "inexpressible gift" of your holy Son (2 Cor. 9:15), who endured being forsaken by you during the moment he became sin for me, that I might become your righteousness and never, in reality, be forsaken by you. In Jesus' name, amen.

MEDITATE MORE

Read in order: Matthew 27:27–50, Psalm 22, and Psalm 23 and ponder the faithfulness of God in the forsakenness of God for your sake.

For you have need of endurance, so that when you have done the will of God you may receive what is promised. HEBREWS 10:36

A Priceless Gift
in a Painful Package

GOD IS FAITHFUL . . . TO INCREASE YOUR ENDURANCE

Not long ago, I met a friend for breakfast. When I asked him how he was doing, he answered, "I'm enduring." This response gave me joy. For many months he'd been wrestling "spiritual forces of evil" (Eph. 6:12) in a fierce, disorienting fight for faith (1 Tim. 6:12). His "enduring," as in working out his faith, indicated that God was at work in him, doing something wonderful (Phil. 2:12).

The New Testament makes it clear that, for the Christian, developing endurance is essential, because "the way is hard that leads to life" (Matt. 7:14), and we're certain to face fiery trials (1 Peter 4:12). Therefore, it says, "you have need of endurance" (Heb. 10:36) because "by your endurance you will gain your lives" (Luke 21:19). God promises to us the "eternal weight of glory" of knowing and being known by Christ (2 Cor. 4:17; Phil. 3:8). But the promise has a crucial condition: *our endurance.*

Our heavenly Father loves to bless his children with good gifts (Luke 11:13). So, when he wants to bless us with the priceless gift of endurance, in what package should we expect it to arrive? One that "seems painful rather than pleasant" (Heb. 12:11): a season of discipline. Because endurance only comes by pushing ourselves (or being pushed) beyond our current limits and persevering through significant, sometimes agonizing, discomfort.

God's discipline can be a confusing gift to receive at first. It was for the original recipients of the epistle to the Hebrews. They too battled spiritual forces of evil, suffering persecution for their faith in Christ and wrestling with their own questions and doubts. They were growing weary and discouraged.

But the author of Hebrews was discerning. He perceived they lacked endurance. Their "drooping hands" and "weak knees" (Heb. 12:12) were putting them at great risk of losing their best and abiding possession (Heb. 10:34). They were losing confidence in Christ and shrinking back in unbelief (Heb. 10:35, 39). These Christians needed encouragement, but not the gentle, consoling kind. They needed exhortation.

So, in love, the writer delivered a clear, strong word: "You have need of endurance, so that when you have done the will of God you may receive what is promised" (Heb. 10:36). He reminded them of the examples set by saints who'd gone before them (Heb. 11), especially the example set by Jesus (Heb. 12:2). And then he reminded them that their affliction was an expression of their Father's faithfulness, a painful package containing his loving gift of endurance—if they'd receive it (Heb. 12:3–11).

We all need this reminder because we all "have need of endurance." And if, in a "severe test of affliction" (2 Cor. 8:2), we're tempted to give up, it's likely we need a firm reminder to "endure hardness, as a good soldier of Jesus Christ" (2 Tim. 2:3 KJV). Because, as Jesus reminded us, "by your endurance you will gain your lives" (Luke 21:19).

It gave me joy that morning at breakfast that my friend needed no such reminder. He was faithfully receiving his faithful Father's very good gift.

PRAYER

Father, thank you for faithfully providing me the endurance I need to receive what you have promised: "fullness of joy" and "pleasures forevermore" in your presence (Ps. 16:11). Give me discernment to recognize this gift in its painful package, and humility to receive a firm exhortation should I begin to lose heart. In Jesus' name, amen.

MEDITATE MORE

Read Hebrews 10:19–12:17. Receive this grace of exhortation if you "have need of endurance," and learn from the writer's firm expression of faithful love if someone you know needs to receive this grace.

The Lord is not slow to fulfill his promise as some count slowness.
2 PETER 3:9

Learn to Trust the Speed of God

GOD IS FAITHFUL . . . EVEN WHEN HE SEEMS SLOW

Your head ages faster than your feet.[4] It's true. Einstein was right. He theorized that the speed of time isn't a constant, as is the speed of light; it's relative to a particular frame of reference. For us, that frame of reference is earth's gravitational force. The higher we are from the earth, the weaker its gravitational pull, and the faster time moves.

This reality impacts us all daily. The GPS[5] satellites we rely on to guide our surface and space vehicles and keep our phones and computers synced orbit in a time different from ours. So, they're programmed to compensate for the time speed differences based on Einstein's calculations. Change the calculations and the result would be catastrophic.

Here's what to keep in mind as we go on: the speed of time we experience in our frame of reference isn't always the speed we should trust. Sometimes it's critically important that we trust a timing based on a different frame of reference.

As Christians, this concept isn't new. Two millennia ago, Peter wrote, "Do not overlook this one fact, beloved, that with the Lord one day is as a thousand years, and a thousand years as one day" (2 Peter 3:8). In other words, in the life of faith it's critically important that we learn to trust God's timing more than our own—to trust the speed of God.

This isn't easy—not only due to sinful unbelief, but because to trust a timing based on a different frame of reference is counterintuitive. Since we can't calculate God's time, his timing often doesn't make sense to us. So, at times we cry, "How long, O LORD?" (Ps. 13:1).

That's why after Peter described a God-day as being like a thousand years for us, he went on to say, "The Lord is not slow to fulfill his promise as some count slowness" (2 Peter 3:9). Indeed. The Creator of light speed, who constantly monitors a universe some 94 billion light-years across, is clearly not slow. But his time scale is clearly very different from ours.

The Creator of time is not constrained by it (Col. 1:16). God is not in time; time is in God (Acts 17:28; Col. 1:17). So, when the speed of God seems slow to us, or when his timing doesn't make sense, we must "not overlook this one fact": God-time is different from human-time. God-time is relative to his purposes, which is his frame of reference. And God, according to his wise purposes, makes "everything beautiful in its time" (Eccl. 3:11)—the time he purposefully chooses for it.

And his purposes, as they relate to us, are beautifully redemptive: "The Lord is not slow . . . but is patient toward [us], not wishing that any should perish, but that all should reach repentance" (2 Peter 3:9).

When God seems slow to us, we must remember that he moves at the speed of his faithfulness to work "all things . . . together for good, for those who are called according to his purpose" (Rom. 8:28). We can trust his timing over the relative and unreliable frame of reference that shapes our expectations.

PRAYER

Father, thank you for being faithful to move at the speed that accomplishes all your purposes (Isa. 46:10) and allows you to make "everything beautiful in its time" (Eccl. 3:11). Forgive me for the times I've questioned your timing in unbelief and teach me to trust your frame of reference over my own. In Jesus' name, amen.

MEDITATE MORE

Read 2 Peter 3. How can you apply what we've just pondered together to the promise of Christ's return?

And he told them a parable to the effect that they ought always to pray and not lose heart. LUKE 18:1

Pray for Your Children and Don't Lose Heart

GOD IS FAITHFUL . . . TO HEAR YOUR PRAYERS FOR YOUR CHILDREN

Years ago, I wrote an article suggesting seven things we parents can pray for our children. However, I included this qualifier:

> Of course, prayers are not magic spells. It's not a matter of just saying the right things and our children will be blessed with success.

> Some parents earnestly pray and their children become gifted leaders or scholars or musicians or athletes. Others earnestly pray and their children develop a serious disability or disease or wander through a prodigal wilderness or just struggle more than others socially or academically or athletically. And the truth is, God is answering all these parents' prayers, but for very different purposes.[6]

This qualifier has become more important to me over time. I've seen children of faithful, prayerful parents reject their parents' faith, and the children of unfaithful parents embrace Christ. I've seen spiritually vibrant young adults become spiritually disillusioned mature adults, and spiritually disillusioned young adults become spiritually vibrant mature adults. The older I get, the less confidence I place in how things appear at any given point. And this has encouraged me to persevere when it comes to praying for my own children.

Like most young parents, my wife and I started out with an almost unconscious assumption that if we parented "right," our kids would embrace the faith we embrace. But years of parenting have humbled me. Our five precious children, all adults now, grew up in the same home, with the same parents who earnestly sought to live out their faith in essentially the same ways, and were part of the same churches. Yet each are walking unique spiritual paths at their own unique speeds. And as of now, not all embrace the faith we tried our insufficient best to nurture. Here is where a parent's faith is tested.

But here is also where a parent can learn to really pray. There's nothing like losing confidence in the power of our abilities to make us more dependent on and desperate for God's power to do for our children what we cannot: give them saving faith. And desperate dependence is what fuels persevering prayer.

That's the lesson of Jesus' parable of the persistent widow in Luke 18. The helpless widow was desperate for justice and dependent on the unrighteous judge to give it to her. Her desperate dependence fueled her relentless petitions till finally the judge granted her request. And if an unrighteous judge can be badgered into granting justice, "will not God give justice to his elect, who cry to him day and night?" (Luke 18:7).

When it comes to our children, Jesus wants us "always to pray and not lose heart" (Luke 18:1). This is a lifelong calling. For if our children are living and doing well spiritually, they are not out of the woods. And if they are living and not doing well spiritually, their story is not over.

God is faithful to hear our prayers for our children. And no matter how, according to his infinitely wise purposes, he determines to answer, he will not allow such a labor to be in vain (1 Cor. 15:58).

PRAYER

Father, thank you for my marvelous children and for faithfully hearing my prayers for them. Increase my awareness of how desperately dependent I am on you to give my children what I cannot, so it will fuel my persistent prayers for them. In Jesus' name, amen.

MEDITATE MORE

Read the parable of the persistent widow in Luke 18:1–8. Why does God value persistence in prayer?

The troubles of my heart are enlarged; bring me out of my distresses.
PSALM 25:17

When Your Heart Is Troubled

GOD IS FAITHFUL . . . TO GUIDE YOU IN TRIBULATION

David was a man of renowned faith-fueled courage, a man who took on lions, bears, giants, and whole armies (1 Sam. 17:36; 19:8). But David didn't always feel full of faith-fueled courage, as many of his psalms reveal.

One example is Psalm 25, where David pleads with God for wisdom and guidance in a desperate moment because "the troubles of [his] heart are enlarged" (Ps. 25:17). And as he does, he models how to pray when we face troubling, perplexing, overwhelming situations and aren't sure what to do.

He begins by *telling God what he needs*. And his first request is for *guidance*:

Make me to know your ways, O LORD; teach me your paths. Lead me in your truth and teach me, for you are the God of my salvation; for you I wait all the day long. (Ps. 25:4–5)

David's troubles were complex, like ours. Crucial things were at stake in how he responded to them, like there are for us. So, he pleaded with God to reveal his ways and lead him in truth, since David's life depended on him (hear the anticipation of John 14:6?).

David's second request is for *forgiveness*:

Remember not the sins of my youth or my transgressions; according to your steadfast love remember me, for the sake of your goodness, O LORD! (Ps. 25:7)

His fearful situation, no doubt, stirred up David's sinful responses, and perhaps memories of past sins. So he humbly confessed them and pleaded for God's mercy.

Then, after telling God what he needs, David *declares what he believes about God*:

Good and upright is the LORD; therefore he instructs sinners in the way. He leads the humble in what is right, and teaches the humble his way. All the paths of the LORD are steadfast love and faithfulness, for those who keep his covenant and his testimonies. (Ps. 25:8–10)

David is helping his "heart take courage" (Ps. 27:14) by confessing his belief in God's faithfulness to do what he promised: to forgive repentant sinners and cause "all the paths" he guides them down lead to their ultimate good (hear the anticipation of Romans 8:28?).

Then, after telling God what he needs, and declaring what he believes about God, David *tells God how he feels.*

Turn to me and be gracious to me, for I am lonely and afflicted. The troubles of my heart are enlarged; bring me out of my distresses. (Ps. 25:16–17)

David, this renowned man of faith-fueled courage, humbles himself like a child and pours out his fearful, weary heart to his heavenly Father. And like all truly valorous saints, he isn't ashamed to do so publicly.

David is a good model here in prayer and spiritual warfare. This warrior knew fear's power to disable us under threat. So in making his requests known to God, he first summoned courage by recalling God's faithfulness and mercy before rehearsing his fears.

And as God did for David, he will also do for us: faithfully instructing us in the way we should choose as we fear him and trust him (Ps. 25:12). And as we do, we too will discover that "all the paths of the LORD are steadfast love and faithfulness" (v. 10).

PRAYER

Father, thank you for faithfully preserving David's prayer in Psalm 25 as one way of making me know your ways and teaching me your paths. When the troubles of my heart are enlarged, encourage my heart with the promise that you will faithfully bring me out of my distresses. In Jesus' name, amen.

MEDITATE MORE

Read all of Psalm 25, and ponder what David meant by verse 14: "The friendship of the LORD is for those who fear him, and he makes known to them his covenant."

When God Doesn't Appear Faithful

GOD IS FAITHFUL . . . IN MOMENTS WHEN IT LEAST APPEARS THAT WAY

According to Luke, these were the very last words Jesus spoke before giving himself over to death. It was a powerful, heartbreaking, poetic moment. The Word of God died with the word of God on his lips, words of poetry, in fact, from the first half of Psalm 31:5. And they were pregnant with more meaning than most hearers realized.

Many Jewish observers on Golgotha that dark afternoon likely knew these words well, having prayed them since childhood just before giving themselves over to sleep at night. But every Jewish religious leader would have also known them as a prayer uttered by a persecuted king of the Jews, and they could have finished the sentence from memory: "You have redeemed me, O LORD, faithful God."

These leaders had been trying to get inside Jesus' head. Who did he think he was? He finally confirmed their suspicions at his trial: he believed himself to be Israel's long-awaited Messiah (Matt. 26:63–64). In quoting David with his last breath, after such brutal torture, had he still believed he was "the son of David" (Matt. 22:41–45)? If so, why? David proved himself the Lord's anointed by God's redeeming him "out of the net" of death (Ps. 31:4). But this so-called Messiah received no such redemption.

Yet, looking at his wasted body hanging on the cross, a sign above him proclaiming him "the King of the Jews" (Matt. 27:37), did any recall more from David's song?

Be gracious to me, O LORD, for I am in distress; my eye is wasted from grief; my soul and my body also. . . . Because of all my adversaries I have become a reproach. (Ps. 31:9, 11)

David, the greatest king of the Jews, had also become a reproach. He'd "been forgotten like one who is dead . . . like a broken vessel" (Ps. 31:12). Had this been in Jesus' mind at the end? David, of course, hadn't died; God delivered and honored him. Surely God would do this and more for the Messiah!

And yet, there was Isaiah's haunting prophecy of the suffering servant who observers would esteem "stricken, smitten by God, and afflicted"; who would be *pierced* for our transgressions; . . . *crushed* for our iniquities" (Isa. 53:4–5); who after being slaughtered like a sacrificial lamb would "prolong his days" (Isa. 53:7–10); whom God would exalt (Isa. 52:13). Had Jesus died believing he was this servant? Had this been why he prophesied his death and resurrection (Matt. 27:62–64)?

Perhaps no one who heard Jesus' final few poetic words pondered these things, and he alone grasped their full meaning. Likely, there was another moment when this was true: "What I am doing you do not understand now, but afterward you will understand" (John 13:7). For almost no one present, even his followers, perceived in Jesus' death history's most profound manifestation of God's faithfulness: to redeem his people from their sins (Matt. 1:21).

And that's one crucial thing Jesus' last prayer means for us. In an agonizing moment, when everything looks wrong, we too can say, "Father, into your hands I commit my spirit," trusting that he will help us understand afterward. Then we too will say, "You have redeemed me, O LORD, faithful God" (Ps. 31:5). For sometimes God is acting most faithfully on our behalf at the moment it least appears that way.

PRAYER

Father, thank you for being most faithful to me through your Son at the moment you appeared least faithful to your Son. Give me faith to pray "Father, into your hands I commit my spirit" in moments I can't see your faithfulness, and to trust that when the time is right, afterward I will understand. In Jesus' name, amen.

MEDITATE MORE

Read John 13:1–17. From the context, what did Jesus mean in verse 7? Are there other areas of your life to which you should apply Jesus' words?

12

And the Lord *God commanded the man, saying, "You may surely eat of every tree of the garden, but of the tree of the knowledge of good and evil you shall not eat, for in the day that you eat of it you shall surely die."* Genesis 2:16-17

God Pursues Your Joy through Every No

God Is Faithful . . . in All His Prohibitions

This was the only prohibition God placed on Adam and Eve in Eden before the horrible fall. They had complete freedom to eat from any tree except the one that would kill their joy.

The prohibition was a way God expressed his profound love for the man and woman that also gave them an opportunity to express their love back to him through trusting and obeying him. It was a liberating prohibition. As long as they believed it was an expression of God's love, it would guard them from becoming slaves of sin (John 8:34) and spare them from the fear of death (Heb. 2:15). It was an expansive restriction, making all the best options for Adam and Eve's enjoyment available to them, as long as they refrained from the one tree.

But they didn't refrain. Instead, they believed the seductive lie that God's prohibition was actually withholding a superior joy from them—becoming "like God, knowing good and evil" (Gen. 3:5). So, they ate the only fruit forbidden them. They transgressed the one gracious law and rejected God's loving no. "Then the eyes of both were opened" (Gen. 3:7), and all hell broke loose. They lost the garden, the incomparable freedom of sinlessness, life without fear of death, and, worst of all, unclouded communion with their heavenly Father. And so did we, through them.

Thank God that wasn't the end of the story. The "last Adam" (1 Cor. 15:45) was sent for us, and he obeyed the Father perfectly for us and paid our full debt of sin so that we, with all who believe in him, will recover an uncursed creation, sinless freedom, eternal life, and, best of all, unclouded, unhindered communion with the triune God. In fact, all who trust and obey Jesus will gain far more than Adam and Eve lost in Eden.

All of God's liberating prohibitions are faithful expressions of his love that give us opportunities to express our faithful love for him through trusting and obeying him. Every one of God's "you shall nots" are expansive restrictions he faithfully places on us so that his "joy may be in [us], and that [our] joy may be full" (John 15:11).

The more we understand this, the more we will understand what the apostle John meant by "There is no fear in love, but perfect love casts out fear" (1 John 4:18). And the more we will understand what the psalmist meant when he wrote, "With the purified you show yourself pure; and with the crooked you make yourself seem tortuous" (Ps. 18:26). For how we interpret God's prohibitions depends on whether we believe that he is pursuing or withholding our greatest joy.

PRAYER

Father, thank you for faithfully pursuing my greatest joy through your loving prohibitions. I believe; and for the sake of my increasing joy in you and your greater glory in me, help my unbelief. In Jesus' name, amen.

MEDITATE MORE

Read John 15:9–11 and then read 1 John 4:18, both through the lens of John 14:15.

13

Truly God is good to Israel, to those who are pure in heart. But as for me, my feet had almost stumbled, my steps had nearly slipped.

PSALM 73:1–2

When Your Foot Nearly Slips

GOD IS FAITHFUL . . . WHEN YOU ENDURE A FAITH CRISIS

Asaph, the composer of this psalm, was a high-profile worship leader in his day. As one of three leaders David chose to oversee the tabernacle's music ministry, he guided many thousands in their worship of God (1 Chron. 15:16–17). Imagine enduring a faith crisis in his position. You don't have to; he wrote a song about it. We know it as Psalm 73.

Many of Israel's great songs proclaimed how God's "work is perfect, for all his ways are justice" (Deut. 32:4), how he "will guard the feet of his faithful ones, but the wicked shall be cut off in darkness" (1 Sam. 2:9), and how "the LORD loves justice; he will not forsake his saints . . . but the . . . wicked shall be cut off" (Ps. 37:28).

However, even as Asaph helped others stand firm on these beliefs, his own faith-feet were slipping. Because in seeing "the prosperity of the wicked," his eyes told him a different story (Ps. 73:2–3). They got wealthier despite being cruel, proud, and blasphemous, and were spared the afflictions and anxieties everyone else suffered (vv. 4–12). Yet Asaph, who could say he'd faithfully "washed [his] hands in innocence," had been "stricken" all day long "and rebuked every morning" (Ps. 73:13–14). God appeared to reward the wicked and punish the righteous, mocking Israel's songs. "All in vain have I kept my heart clean," he thought (v. 13). Asaph's faith was in crisis.

Then one day, when he "went into the sanctuary of God" (v. 17), something happened that changed everything. It wasn't a sudden change in the worldly fortunes of the wicked; it was a sudden change in Asaph's perspective on reality. The Spirit of wisdom and of revelation enlightened the eyes of his heart to know the hope to which he was called (Eph. 1:17–18). And these eyes told him a different story than the eyes in his head.

Asaph understood the end of the wicked, "how they are destroyed in a moment, swept away utterly by terrors!" (Ps. 73:17–19)—the terrible end of "everyone who is unfaithful to [God]" (v. 27). And he discerned in all the strikes, rebukes, and privations he'd received, God was faithfully guiding him with his counsel so that afterward God would receive him to glory (vv. 23–24)—the glorious end of everyone who is faithful to God. Asaph's cynical doubt turned to humble faith and his bitter complaint to grateful praise:

> Whom have I in heaven but you? And there is nothing on earth that I desire besides you. My flesh and my heart may fail, but God is the strength of my heart and my portion forever. (vv. 25–26)

God preserved Asaph's testimony to remind us in our faith crises that he "knows how to rescue the godly from trials" (2 Peter 2:9). And he knows *when* to rescue us. If your faith-feet begin to slip because the eyes in your head tell you a cynical, faithless story, keep seeking him. God will be faithful to enlighten the eyes of your heart to see that the real story is far bigger, far better, and abounding in hope (Rom. 15:13).

PRAYER

Father, thank you for your faithfulness to Asaph and what it means about your faithfulness to me. When my foot is slipping, lead me to the "sanctuary" of your choosing, restore my spiritual sight, and fill me with "all joy and peace in believing, so that by the power of the Holy Spirit" I "may abound in hope" (Rom. 15:13). In Jesus' name, amen.

MEDITATE MORE

Read all of Psalm 73 and pray through verses 25–26 until you taste the sweetness of the hope they express.

He began to cry out and say, "Jesus, Son of David, have mercy on me!" MARK 10:47

What Do You Want?

GOD IS FAITHFUL . . . TO ANSWER PREVAILING PRAYER

Bartimaeus was blind. And his soul-weariness over it was beyond description. As soon as he'd realized Jesus, the great Healer, was passing by, he'd begun shouting. He did not want the Son of David to pass him by.

His first shouts got no response from Jesus. But they did get many "Be quiets!" from voices around him. Bartimaeus wasn't about to be quiet, though, not when the one person with the power to restore his sight was this close. This was no time for politeness, no time for the passive fatalism of "I guess God just doesn't listen to me." He was desperate and going to be heard. He shouted louder: "Son of David, have mercy on me!"

Finally, a friendly voice said, "Take heart. Get up; he is calling you." Bartimaeus leaped up and a friendly hand guided him forward. Then a strong, gentle voice spoke: "What do you want me to do for you?" Bartimaeus, trembling, now made his desperate request with deference: "Rabbi, let me recover my sight."

There was a silent pause. Bartimaeus's heart was pounding. Then the strong, gentle voice spoke again: "Go your way; your faith has made you well."

Before the words had finished, Bartimaeus felt a strange sensation in his eyes. Revived optical nerves detected first brightness, then swimming images. Could it be? His tear ducts began to overflow, both to lubricate the conjunctiva and to express a grateful joy just dawning after darkness. As his pupils contracted from the brilliance of the midday sun, Bartimaeus rubbed his eyes. When he opened them again, he was looking into the intense eyes of a young man.

Bartimaeus is a kind of picture of prevailing prayer, when we so desperately want God to do something for us that we won't stop asking until he answers. And God encourages us to pray this way. We see this in Jesus' parable when the widow persists in nagging the unrighteous judge until he gives her what she wants (Luke 18:1–8). This is precisely the determination God wants us to bring to prayer. He's looking for those who will "always . . . pray and not lose heart," for those willing to "cry to him day and night," for desperate Bartimaeus-like prayers who will insist on being heard and won't take a non-response for an answer.

Why? Because he's looking to "find faith on earth" (Luke 18:8). Desperation in us often calls forth faith in us. And having to persist in desperate prayer builds faith with fortitude—endurance. And faith that persists demonstrates to us and those who observe us that we really believe God can do what we're asking. That kind of faith honors God.

And God will be faithful to his promise to "speedily" give "justice" to his prayerfully persistent elect (Luke 18:8). We'll trust him to determine what "speedily" and "justice" should look like for us. For our part, let us determine to be heard, to nag him incessantly in faith, night and day, if necessary, until he answers us. God loves that kind of faith.

PRAYER

Father, thank you for Bartimaeus's desperate, faith-fueled audacity to insist on Jesus answering him. Teach me to pray like this, for I want to be one in whom you "find faith on the earth." In Jesus' name, amen.

MEDITATE MORE

Read Luke 18:1–8.

| *He has made everything beautiful in its time.* ECCLESIASTES 3:11

He Will Bring Beauty from Your Bygone Shadow

GOD IS FAITHFUL . . . TO REDEEM YOUR PAINFUL PAST

In the small front yard of our Minneapolis home live two crabapple trees, one on the north side and one on the south. We planted them on the same day over two decades ago, and for seven years they looked very similar as they grew.

Then a mulberry tree began to grow in our south-side neighbors' hedge, not far from the south crab. The neighbors moved and the mulberry tree grew amazingly fast. Soon the crab found itself in the mulberry's shadow. In order to survive, the crab was forced to struggle upward for the life-giving light it desperately needed. After a number of years, the mulberry was removed. But the effect its shadow had on the south-side crab was lasting. It had grown nearly twice as tall as the other crab, and most of its branches extended up rather than out, giving it an odd look, especially compared to its north-side sister.

Today, more than a decade after the mulberry's removal, both trees are mature and beautiful. The north-side one is a model crab, twenty feet tall and beautifully proportioned. The south-side crab has also become beautifully proportioned. But it's far taller, at least forty feet, and much fuller, producing far more berries to nourish the birds who have to survive a Minnesota winter. And this is because, in its past, it had been forced to struggle for light in the mulberry's shadow.

Perhaps you've had a "mulberry" in your past. It may be gone now, but it shaped you in ways you wouldn't have chosen, and those effects remain. Perhaps, like the crab in the years following the mulberry's removal, your dimensions are disproportionate, giving you an odd look compared to other trees in the garden of God, and you're painfully conscious of this.

One way to understand your unique "shape" is that it reflects how you struggled for life-giving light when you were younger—a challenge other young trees didn't face. While it was there, the "mulberry" cast a shadow over you and, in order to survive, you had to push toward the light in ways you wouldn't have without it. You did this because that's how you're designed: to push toward the light.

But your Creator, who makes "everything beautiful in its time" (Eccl. 3:11), will be faithful to make you beautiful in your time. Your Redeemer, who works all things together for good for those who love him and are called according to his purpose (Rom. 8:28), will be faithful to redeem the effect of the mulberry shadow in your past and cause you to bear fruit that will nourish others, especially those with mulberry shadows in their past (2 Cor. 1:3–4).

And if you're struggling right now in the shadow of a mulberry, take heart: your Redeemer is the great Remover of mulberry trees (Luke 17:6). And he who came to "give light to those who sit in darkness" (Luke 1:79) will be faithful to shine on you and, like our beautiful south-side crab, make you beautiful in your time.

PRAYER

Father, thank you for your promise to make everything beautiful in its time. I trust you to be faithful to cause the effects of my past shadows to work for beautiful good according to your purposes, for my joy and your glory. In Jesus' name, amen.

MEDITATE MORE

Read John 9. What beauty did Jesus bring from the shadow of the man's past suffering?

Every Hour, I Need Thee!

GOD IS FAITHFUL . . . TO TEACH YOU TO PRAY

When the disciples asked Jesus to teach them to pray, they were requesting something other rabbis taught their disciples: a practical model for what to pray (a category template) and how to pray it (a structural template). And Jesus was faithful to provide this in the Lord's Prayer (Luke 11:2–4); it teaches us *how* to pray.

But the Lord's Prayer doesn't teach us *to pray*—to actually do it. What teaches us *to pray* is need—knowing how much we need God. But I don't mean knowing *in theory* how much we need God. Many who have a strong theology of prayer struggle to actually pray. By *knowing* our need for God, I mean deeply *feeling* our need for him. Even those with a weak theology of prayer will struggle *not* to pray when they feel desperate for God's help.

That's why, when we're lacking motivation to pray, trying a new prayer technique or system typically only helps as long as its novelty lasts. The solution for complacent prayerlessness is not a new method but a new awareness of our need. So, this is what we should be praying: "Lord, teach me *to pray*." The Lord loves when we yearn to desire him more and depend on him more, and he is faithful to answer this prayer. And when he does, it will likely come in the form of desperation.

You might not recognize it as an answered prayer at first. It will get you praying, but you'll be praying for God to deliver you from what's making you desperate for him. That's not wrong. He tells us, "Call upon me in the day of trouble; I will deliver you, and you shall glorify me" (Ps. 50:15). But when God is teaching you *to pray*, the desperation usually lasts longer than you would like. However, at some point, you'll notice that you've been praying more and with more faith, that Scripture has been more vibrant, and that you're more spiritually engaged all-around. Why? Because your deeply felt need for God has driven you to him. And the preciousness of God's gift of desperation will begin to dawn.

Desperation certainly is not the last word on prayer. God wants us to come to him "in *everything*" (Phil. 4:6), not just desperate need. But it's usually the first word on prayer. Because unless real need is felt, real prayer rarely occurs.

And since need drives us to prayer, a sustained heightened sense of our need for God is what makes it possible to "pray without ceasing" (1 Thess. 5:17). And, as saints through the centuries have testified, it *is* possible. For if we ask him, the Lord, who is faithful to teach us *to pray* by giving us a heightened sense of how much we need him, will also be faithful to teach us *to pray without ceasing* by making that heightened sense an unceasing sense, leading us to say with the hymn writer, "I need Thee, oh, I need Thee! Every hour I need Thee!"[7]

PRAYER

Lord, "I need Thee, oh, I need Thee! Every hour I need Thee!" And where I need a heightened sense of my desperate need for you, grant this to me. I trust your steadfast love for me as you faithfully do what you must to teach me to pray. In Jesus' name, amen.

MEDITATE MORE

Read Ephesians 6:10–18. According to Paul, what understanding of reality must we have in order to sustain our unceasing sense of need for God, driving us to pray "at all times in the Spirit" (Eph. 6:18)? How keenly do you feel this reality?

17

"Simon, Simon, behold, Satan demanded to have you, that he might sift you like wheat, but I have prayed for you that your faith may not fail. And when you have turned again, strengthen your brothers." LUKE 22:31-32

Jesus' Devastating Mercy

GOD IS FAITHFUL . . . TO GIVE YOU THE MERCY YOU MOST NEED

Jesus spoke these words during his final Passover with the Twelve, not long after announcing that one of them would betray him. That news shocked and grieved Peter, and left him reeling. "When you have *turned again*"? That implied he was going to *turn away* from Jesus. Never! Not even if everyone else did (Matt. 26:33). He declared in protest, "Lord, I am ready to go with you both to prison and to death" (Luke 22:33).

Jesus knew Peter was sincere, but self-deceived. He couldn't see his misplaced self-confidence. So, Jesus dropped the bomb: "I tell you, Peter, the rooster will not crow this day, until you deny three times that you know me" (Luke 22:34). Peter simply couldn't imagine doing such a thing. Again, he vowed, "I will not deny you" (Mark 14:31).

Then, in just a matter of hours, Jesus' prophecy came to pass. All it took was a servant girl's public accusation and this man who swore his loyal love to the death found himself swearing the inconceivable: "I do not know him" (Luke 22:57). After two more denials, a rooster crowed. Peter was devastated.

But this devastating moment of failure turned out to be an immense mercy to Peter. What Peter needed was true spiritual strength—what he would later call "the strength that God supplies" (1 Peter 4:11)—for the future assignment Jesus had for him. But he first needed to know how weak he was without it, how susceptible he was to his sin nature. Jesus' faithful prayer strengthened Peter more than he likely knew, keeping his faith from ultimately failing. And in God's mercy, this failure didn't define Peter, it disciplined him.

We all, in our unique ways, need to be devastated by Jesus' merciful love. And when he loves us in this way, it's a manifestation of his faithfulness. "The Lord disciplines the one he loves" (Heb. 12:6), and he knows what we need in order to ultimately fill us with his joy (John 15:11) and make us most fruitful in the assignments he has for us (John 15:5).

After allowing Peter to be mercifully devastated, Jesus mercifully restored him after another meal—a post-resurrection breakfast on a beach (John 21:15–19). Jesus asked him three times a version of this question: "Simon, son of John, do you love me?" Three merciful, wonderful opportunities for Peter to affirm his love for his Lord—one for every terrible, unloving denial.

As Jesus faithfully restored Peter after his failure, he will faithfully and mercifully restore us after ours. And Peter's painful, humbling experience equipped him to pastor us through our experiences of Jesus' devastating mercy, which he does through these words: "After you have suffered a little while, the God of all grace, who has called you to his eternal glory in Christ, will himself restore, confirm, strengthen, and establish you" (1 Peter 5:10).

PRAYER

Father, thank you for being "the God of all grace," including your faithful disciplining grace that for the moment is "painful rather than pleasant" (Heb. 12:11), for I trust that when it has done its sanctifying, equipping work, you will faithfully "restore, confirm, strengthen, and establish" me and increase my fruitfulness in the assignments you give me. In Jesus' name, amen.

MEDITATE MORE

Read John 21:15–19, the story of Peter's restoration, and consider how his "sifting" experience equipped him for the assignment Jesus was giving him.

18

I know, O LORD, that your rules are righteous, and that in faithfulness you have afflicted me. PSALM 119:75

In Faithfulness
You Have Afflicted Me

GOD IS FAITHFUL . . . WHEN YOU'RE PRONE TO WANDER

In our day, this is a remarkable thing to say *about* God, much less *to* God: "in faithfulness you have afflicted me." Many professing Christians are troubled by the thought that a loving God would afflict them. They're even more troubled when they realize that this psalmist's "severe" affliction (Ps. 119:107) came through ungodly, powerful people cruelly mistreating him (v. 161).

Was the psalmist really saying that God used evil agents to faithfully afflict him? Yes. This might offend modern sensibilities, but it didn't offend biblical sensibilities. Throughout the Scriptures, we see God lovingly and faithfully accomplish good for his people through evil agents. In fact, his supreme act of love and faithfulness was displayed when, through the actions of evil agents, he accomplished the greatest good for his people by giving his only Son to die on the cross in their place.

So, what faithful good was God doing for this psalmist? Here's what he said: "Before I was afflicted I went astray, but now I keep your word" (v. 67). And again, "It is good for me that I was afflicted, that I might learn your statutes" (v. 71). As one who believed in God's sovereignty over all things (vv. 89–90) and God's goodness in all things (v. 68), he was able to discern in his suffering, even at the hands of evil agents, that God was lovingly correcting his proneness to wander. Therefore, he was able to say, "This is my comfort in my affliction, that your promise gives me life" (v. 50). He found comfort both in God's promise to do him good through his affliction, and God's promise to ultimately deliver him from it.

As a result, the psalmist grew to love God's word "exceedingly" (v. 167). It became "the sum of [all] truth" to him (v. 160), "a light to [his] path" (v. 105), and his refuge when he felt threatened (v. 114). So, he meditated on it throughout the day (v. 97) and found it "sweeter than honey" (v. 103) and more valuable than gold (v. 72).

God's purposes in our afflictions are always redemptive (Rom. 8:28). And sometimes, as it was for this poet, they are God's counterintuitive ways of faithfully fulfilling his promise to us:

> "I will put the fear of me in their hearts, that they may not turn from me. I will rejoice in doing them good . . . with all my heart and all my soul." (Jer. 32:40–41)

The more we see God's faithfulness in our afflictions, the more we will join Paul in his praise, "Blessed be the God and Father of our Lord Jesus Christ, the Father of mercies and God of all comfort, who comforts us in all our affliction" (2 Cor. 1:3–4). Because we realize, with Paul and this psalmist, that included in the "all" of "the God of all comfort" is the comfort that God, in his steadfast love, has in faithfulness afflicted us.

PRAYER

Father, thank you for pursuing me with "goodness and mercy . . . all the days of my life" (Ps. 23:6), even when in faithfulness you afflict me. Help me discern when that's happening and to remember that it's one way you are doing me good with all your heart and all your soul. In Jesus' name, amen.

MEDITATE MORE

Read through Psalm 119 and note how the psalmist was able to discern both God's good purposes in his affliction and honestly express the grief over the injustice he was suffering and the toll it was taking on him. How well are you able to live in the tension of "as sorrowful, yet always rejoicing" (2 Cor. 6:10)?

"Naked I came from my mother's womb, and naked shall I return. The LORD gave, and the LORD has taken away; blessed be the name of the LORD." JOB 1:21

What God Gives
through Your Losses

GOD IS FAITHFUL . . . EVEN WHEN HE TAKES AWAY

From time immemorial people have known that what we really love and trust is often revealed when we are tested by loss. So has Satan. Which is why, regarding Job, he argued to God:

> "Does Job fear God for no reason? Have you not put a hedge around him and his house and all that he has, on every side? You have blessed the work of his hands, and his possessions have increased in the land. But stretch out your hand and touch all that he has, and he will curse you to your face." (Job 1:9–11)

Satan argued from experience, having watched thousands suffer loss and curse God. So, God gave Satan permission to take away most of Job's worldly loves and blessings.

Now, let's heed Jesus' words, "Do not judge by appearances, but judge with right judgment" (John 7:24). As John Piper says, "God is always doing 10,000 things in your life, and you may be aware of three of them."[8] Given all Scripture reveals of God's character and purposes, we're wise to assume God was doing far more than participating in a divine wager.

How did Job respond? "Naked I came from my mother's womb, and naked shall I return. The LORD gave, and the LORD has taken away; blessed be the name of the LORD" (Job 1:21).

Satan was proven wrong about Job. But he wasn't wrong about the concealing power of prosperity and the revealing power of loss. So, since his aim is to "steal and kill and destroy" the faith of Christians (John 10:10), he may seek to take away God's "blessings" if he thinks this loss may result in our loss of faith. But if he thinks prosperity will corrupt our faith, or conceal our false faith, Satan may, as he tried with Jesus, offer us the world (Luke 4:5–7).

But Jesus' aim is to give us true "treasure in heaven" (Mark 10:21) and true "pleasures forevermore" (Ps. 16:11). That's why he requires us to deny ourselves and take up our crosses (Matt. 16:24), and sometimes he calls us to leave homes, land, family, and vocations for his sake and the gospel's (Mark 10:29). Because, when for Christ's sake we are willing to count as loss what the world counts as gain, Christ is revealed to be gain to us (Phil. 3:8).

And when, in his wise providence, he allows precious people and valued possessions to be taken away from us, one of his ten thousand purposes might be to "put . . . to open shame" evil powers (Col. 2:15) and reveal to a watching world the One we consider supremely precious and the better, abiding possession he offers (Heb. 10:34).

God is faithful and blessed in both what he gives to and takes away from us, because he does both for the sake of our (and perhaps countless others') ultimate, eternal joy. And sometimes his most precious gifts come through painful losses.

PRAYER

Father, thank you for being faithful and blessed in both what you give and what you take away. Deliver me from the thief that steals, kills, and destroys, but do not allow prosperity to conceal idolatry in me. And should I suffer the loss of all things, grant that Christ will be gain to me (Phil. 3:8) that is "better than life" (Ps. 63:3). In Jesus' name, amen.

MEDITATE MORE

Read Philippians 3:7–11 and ponder what Paul gained, having "suffered the loss of all things" (v. 8).

20

Not only that, but we rejoice in our sufferings, knowing that suffering produces endurance, and endurance produces character, and character produces hope. ROMANS 5:3–4

Assurance Comes through Spiritual Struggle

GOD IS FAITHFUL . . . TO GIVE YOU THE FULL ASSURANCE OF FAITH

Am I truly a Christian? Few questions cause more fearful trembling in believers. And few soul-shepherds are as helpful as John Newton (1725–1807) in explaining to trembling saints how God faithfully assures them of their "calling and election" (2 Peter 1:10):

> Assurance grows by repeated conflict, by our repeated experimental proof of the Lord's power and goodness to save; when we have been brought very low and helped, sorely wounded and healed, cast down and raised again, have given up all hope, and been suddenly snatched from danger, and placed in safety; and when these things have been repeated to us and in us a thousand times over, we begin to learn to trust simply to the word and power of God, beyond and against appearances: and this trust, when habitual and strong, bears the name of assurance; for even assurance has degrees.[9]

Why does God choose to give us a growing assurance through enduring trials? Newton answers this way: "We cannot be safely trusted with assurance till we have that knowledge of the evil and deceitfulness of our hearts, which can be acquired only by painful, repeated experience."[10]

Like Peter, who vowed he'd never deny Jesus only hours before he did (Matt. 26:35), we often don't realize how proud and self-reliant we are and how weak our faith is until we're placed into the heat of fiery trials, and the dross of fear and unbelief rise to the surface. And when we see the dross, we can fear that our faith may not be real.

But paradoxically, this is often where God begins to increase our assurance. For seeing the power of our indwelling sin and feeling our helplessness to escape it on our own pushes us in desperation to trust Christ's work on the cross alone. When we see how weak we are and feel our helplessness to be strong on our own, it pushes us to search out and trust Christ's promises to us. This was Newton's experience: "In mercy he [God] has frequently stirred up my nest, shaken me in it, and forced me to fly to him, when I should otherwise have dropped into sleep and [false] security."[11]

God wants our faith to rest fully on the rock of Christ so that we "rely not on ourselves but on God who raises the dead" (2 Cor. 1:9). Because, as Newton said, "We are never more safe, never have more reason to expect the Lord's help, than when we are most sensible that we can do nothing without him."[12]

God loves to give his children the gift of the "full assurance of faith" (Heb. 10:22). And he is faithful to give us this gift, not through an unreliable, subjective inner witness vulnerable to our fickle, fluctuating emotions, but through various kinds of trials and sufferings. For "suffering produces endurance, and endurance produces character, and character produces hope" (Rom. 5:3–4). Greater assurance comes through stronger faith. And faith only grows stronger through the vigorous exercise of testing.

PRAYER

Father, thank you for wanting me to experience the full assurance of faith, and for giving me this precious gift through the repeated testing of my faith, which produces endurance, which produces character, which produces assuring hope (Rom. 5:3–4). Help me, therefore, to count these testings "all joy" (James 1:2). In Jesus' name, amen.

MEDITATE MORE

Read Hebrews 12:7–11. According to the author, what yields "the peaceful fruit of righteousness" in the life of a Christian? Also see Romans 5:3–4.

21

For we are his workmanship, created in Christ Jesus for good works, which God prepared beforehand, that we should walk in them. EPHESIANS 2:10

You Are God's Masterpiece

GOD IS FAITHFUL . . . IN HOW AND WHY HE CREATED YOU

According to this verse, you are a living poem. If that comes off like a schmaltzy caption on an inspirational poster, hear me out.

The Greek word for "workmanship" in this verse is *poiēma*, and you don't need to know Greek to see this is where we get our English word "poem." But what Paul had in mind was a work of masterful creativity. So, if you think of poetry, think of Homer's *Odyssey* or Dante's *Divine Comedy* or Milton's *Paradise Lost* or Spenser's *Faerie Queene*—great epic masterpieces.

Paul selected this word carefully. The only other time he used *poiēma* was in Romans 1:20: "For his invisible attributes, namely, his eternal power and divine nature, have been clearly perceived, ever since the creation of the world, in the *things that have been made*"—those last five words translating *poiēma*. All that we see, hear, touch, taste, and smell in the universe is reading God's epic masterpiece. Homer, Dante, Milton, and Spenser were master poets, but the characters in their poems are imagined, not *real*. When God imagines, his images become *real*—his poems become living and active and multidimensional.

What God through Paul wants you to understand is this: You are an epic, God-imaging poem become flesh and spirit, containing all the comedic and tragic drama of an existence more real and meaningful than you've yet comprehended. If you're tempted to think God must have had an off day when he composed you, you don't yet see things as they really are.

In cosmic terms, you appear infinitesimally small and ephemeral. Yet, you are more glorious than the sun and more fascinating than Orion. For the sun can't perceive its Creator's power in its own blinding glory, and Orion can't trace his Designer's genius in the precision of his heavenly course. But you can. You are among the infinitesimally few creations God has granted the incredible capacity for self-consciousness *and* God-consciousness. And to no one else has he given your unique perception and experience of *things that have been made*—his holy, grand *poiēma*. To no one else has he given your unique part to play in his cosmic epic. This is not inspirational poster kitsch; this is biblical reality.

Wonder at this: God has faithfully prepared just for you what he's given you to do (Eph. 2:10). Nothing you do today is unimportant. God is keenly interested in the smallest detail. You don't need a more wonderful calling; you may just need more strength to comprehend the wonder of his loving ways toward you (Eph. 3:17–19).

Today you get the priceless privilege of reading with your whole being one verse or maybe a few lines in the great *poiēma* of God, while at the same time being a *poiēma* yourself, a work of master creativity that God faithfully composed and will faithfully remember and recite forever.

PRAYER

Father, thank you for the priceless gifts of life and consciousness that make it possible to utter this prayer. Thank you for creating me in the way you have and for giving me my unique part to play at this time and place in your cosmic poiēma, all which you faithfully "prepared beforehand" just for me according to your wise and gracious purposes. Forgive me for so often questioning your wisdom and doubting your graciousness. Give me strength today to comprehend your love for me and to steward well all that you've graciously entrusted to me. In Jesus' name, amen.

MEDITATE MORE

Read Ephesians 2:1–10 and allow the Spirit through Paul's words to remind you what God has done to make the *poiēma* of your life so extraordinarily wonderful.

22

"You will know the truth, and the truth will set you free."
JOHN 8:32

For All the Knots You Can't Untie

GOD IS FAITHFUL ... TO SET YOU FREE WITH HIS TRUTH

A Gordian knot is a problem so complex, no one can figure it out. Have you ever wondered where that term came from?

According to legend,[13] once upon a time in ancient Phrygia (now central Turkey), an oracle prophesied that the next man to drive an oxcart into the capital city would be king. That man was a peasant farmer named Gordios. His son Midas (of later golden-touch fame), who'd accompanied him, dedicated the auspicious oxcart to Zeus and tied it to a pole in the temple using a knot so complex it was considered impossible to untie—the Gordian knot. Another oracle prophesied that whoever solved the riddle of the knot would rule Asia. Centuries later, when Alexander the Great arrived in the city, he entered the temple of Zeus, heard the prophecy, and tried his hand at the knot. Failing to untie it, he drew his sword and sliced through it. He then went on to conquer Asia.

We all have Gordian-like knots we can't untie: complex intellectual, spiritual, emotional, and psychological entanglements of our indwelling sin, constitutional weaknesses, disabilities, circumstantial adversities, complicated relationships, and traumatic past experiences. We try to untangle them, but the more we try, the more complex we find the knots to be. With some knots, counseling and therapy can help us cope, but they can't fully untie them, and we cry out with Paul, "Wretched man that I am! Who will deliver me from this body of death?" (Rom. 7:24). Who can untie these sin-permeated, hopelessly intertwined knots of pain? No earthly expert can. Nor can we fashion a sword sharp enough to cut through them.

But there is one who can solve the riddle of our Gordian knots. "He is called ... The Word of God" and "from his mouth comes a sharp sword" (Rev. 19:13, 15). He is the prophesied conqueror who, upon arriving in the city, faithfully dealt the decisive sword blow on every fall-induced Gordian knot of sin and futility binding every saint who would ever belong to him. And he is the "Wonderful Counselor" (Isa. 9:6) who calls us to bring him all that burdens us (Matt. 11:28) and comforts our troubled hearts with these words, "Believe in God; believe also in me" (John 14:1)—promising to those who do, "You will know the truth, and the truth will set you free" (John 8:32).

Freedom from our Gordian knots is not ultimately found by exploring the labyrinthian caves of our psyche, but in wielding the "living and active" "sword of the Spirit, which is the word of God" (Heb. 4:12; Eph. 6:17). He is the living Word (John 1:1) and he is "Faithful and True" (Rev. 19:11). He is the truth (John 14:6), who will set free all who believe in him; the Conqueror who will make us "more than conquerors" (Rom. 8:37).

PRAYER

Father, thank you for sending your faithful, conquering Son to cut through my Gordian knots of sin and futility with his sword of truth and set me free. Give me grace today to believe in you, and also in him, by casting all my anxieties on you (1 Peter 5:7) and not trying to untie impossible knots by leaning on my own understanding. In Jesus' name, amen.

MEDITATE MORE

Review Philippians 4:6–7 as a practical way of entrusting your impossible knots to your faithful Creator (1 Peter 4:19).

23

What I am doing you do not understand now, but afterward you will understand. JOHN 13:7

Afterward You Will Understand

GOD IS FAITHFUL . . . WHEN HE WITHHOLDS INFORMATION FROM US

This is one of numerous profound, important things Jesus said to his disciples the night before his crucifixion. But it's one we might overlook, given its context.

During that final Passover meal, Jesus stripped down like a servant and proceeded to wash each disciple's feet. This might not shock us two millennia removed and familiar with this story. But it shocked Peter. The more he watched the "Son of the living God" (Matt. 16:16) using his own holy hands to wash the uncleanness off their feet, the more indignant he felt. All his life, he'd understood foot-washing as a demeaning task far beneath the dignity of honored men. So, when Jesus got to him, Peter pulled his feet back. "Lord, do you wash my feet?" (John 13:6). Jesus patiently responded to his earnest disciple, "What I am doing you do not understand now, but afterward you will understand" (v. 7).

And there it is: a massively important principle for every Christian's life of faith: a summary of a motif woven throughout Scripture from beginning to end, captured in a simple reply to a perplexed disciple's question.

Peter was in the good company of many great saints who didn't understand what God was doing in a confusing moment, only to understand later. Think of Abraham preparing to sacrifice Isaac, after having waited so long for him (Gen. 22); or Joseph languishing for years in an Egyptian prison because he'd been faithful to God (Gen. 37–41); or Gideon getting three hundred warriors ready to attack an innumerable army of Midianites (Judg. 7); or Martha and Mary burying their brother, wondering why Jesus hadn't come (John 11)—just to name a few.

Finding Jesus' *trust now/understand later* explanation insufficient, Peter declared, "You shall never wash my feet" (John 13:8). His response was well-intended, but wrongheaded. In trying not to dishonor his Lord, that's precisely what he did. For the dishonor wasn't in washing Peter's uncleanness, it was in Peter's not trusting what Jesus said. So, Jesus' response was very serious: "If I do not wash you, you have no share with me" (John 13:8). *Distrust now meant exclusion.* Peter got the point immediately and repented by exclaiming, "Lord, not my feet only but also my hands and my head!" (John 13:9).

We often do not understand what God is doing in a confusing moment. And the crucial truth is, we don't need to understand *then* to follow him in faith. When God asks us to trust him now and understand him later, he is being a wise, faithful Father. Sometimes his reasons have to do with his timing, as it did for Peter. And sometimes, because God's ways and thoughts are so beyond ours (Isa. 55:8–9), he withholds from us knowledge we're not strong enough to bear yet, and so is mercifully bearing it for us.

We are never on more dangerous ground than when we believe we understand better than God. But if we will trust him now, afterward, when the time is right in the near or distant future, he will faithfully give us all the understanding we need.

PRAYER

Father, thank you for being faithful in both the understanding you give me and in the understanding you withhold from me. Teach me to trust you, as you did my forebears in the faith, whenever you call me to trust you now and understand later. In Jesus' name, amen.

MEDITATE MORE

Read Hebrews 11:8–16. What was God's promise that fueled Abraham and others to trust God when they didn't know where they were going? What's God's promise that fuels your walking by faith, not by sight?

24

"If you know these things, blessed are you if you do them."
JOHN 13:17

Love with Aggressive Grace

GOD IS FAITHFUL . . . TO NOT LET YOU MERELY "KNOW THESE THINGS"

In recent years, I have grieved as I watched relationships between Christians I love dearly break apart, not over major doctrinal differences or gross immorality, but over relational conflicts. I saw offending parties refuse to receive needed correction, and offended parties refuse to receive offending parties' efforts to reconcile. Each case had its complexities, but over all of them flew the banner of these words of Jesus: "By this all people will know that you are my disciples, if you have love for one another" (John 13:35). If Christians can't or won't reconcile, what does it say about Jesus' love?

As Christians, we know "God is love" (1 John 4:16). We know that love is the sum of the Law and the Prophets (Matt. 22:37–40), that love moved the Father to give his only Son (John 3:16), and that love moved the Son to lay down his life for his friends for the glory of his Father (John 15:13; 17:4). We know that nothing is more godlike, nothing gives God more glory and delight, nothing is more morally beautiful, profoundly meaningful, and joy-producing in the human experience, and nothing is more offensive, violent, or destructive to the forces of darkness than love. *We know this.*

But as Jesus said, "If you know these things, blessed are you if you do them" (John 13:17). *Knowing* isn't enough; the whole blessing of love is in the *doing* of love. If we know what love is, but don't do what love does, we are nothing and gain nothing (1 Cor. 13:1–3).

In Romans 12, Paul describes what this distinctly Christian love looks like in action:

Love one another with [genuine] brotherly affection. (v. 10)

Outdo one another in showing honor. (v. 10)

Rejoice with those who rejoice, weep with those who weep. (v. 15)

Never be wise in your own sight. (v. 16)

Repay no one evil for evil, but give thought to do what is honorable in the sight of all. (v. 17)

If possible, so far as it depends on you, live peaceably with all. (v. 18)

This is what aggressively gracious, faithful, costly Calvary looks like. I call it "aggressive grace" for two reasons. First, we are called to love one another, not as we deserve, but as Jesus loved us—with shocking, remarkably *gracious* love (John 15:12). Second, it's *aggressive* because it's a remarkably pursuing, persevering, pride-slaying, overcoming love. This is love that overcomes evil with good (Rom. 12:21). This is Jesus-like love the world is meant to recognize in his disciples.

This love is easy to know and talk about, but hard to do. Yes, Calvary was hard. But the stakes are high. For if we will not overcome evil with good, we will be overcome by evil. But if we will seek to love one another as Jesus loved us (John 15:12), God, who faithfully loved and pursued us with aggressive grace "while we were enemies" (Rom. 5:10), will be faithful to provide us the aggressive grace we need.

We know these things. But knowing isn't enough. Blessed are we if we do them.

PRAYER

Father, thank you for so faithfully pursuing me with such an aggressively gracious love. Forgive me for all the times I have known how I should love my fellow Christians and failed in the doing of that love. Whatever it takes, let me be one through whom non-Christians can observe the love of Jesus, in whose name I pray, amen.

MEDITATE MORE

Read Romans 12, and honestly assess yourself against each statement in verses 9–12. How well are you helping to foster a culture of aggressive grace in your local church?

25

Finally, be strong in the Lord and in the strength of his might. Put on the whole armor of God, that you may be able to stand against the schemes of the devil. EPHESIANS 6:10-11

Do You Know What Hunts You?

GOD IS FAITHFUL . . . TO HELP YOU TAKE SPIRITUAL WARFARE SERIOUSLY

In Peter Jackson's film adaptation of J. R. R. Tolkien's *The Fellowship of the Ring*, after the hobbit Frodo's first encounters with the evil Nazgûl, he meets Strider, who is actually King Aragorn in disguise. Strider asks Frodo, "Are you frightened?" Frodo answers, "Yes." Strider replies, "Not nearly frightened enough. I know what hunts you."[14]

You are, no doubt, aware that, as Christians, we're being pursued by "spiritual forces of evil in the heavenly places" (Eph. 6:12). The question is, Are you appropriately "frightened enough"? Do you know what hunts you?

"The devil and his angels" (Matt. 25:41) factored prominently in Jesus' life, teaching, and miracles. Jesus taught that Satan sees the world as his "kingdom" (Luke 11:17–18) and that demons enslave people (Luke 13:16), gain influence over religious leaders and institutions (John 8:44), and oppose, undermine, and corrupt gospel ministry (Luke 8:12). So, Jesus made a particular focus of his ministry "healing all who were oppressed by the devil" (Acts 10:38).

Then Jesus commissioned his apostles "to open [unbelievers'] eyes, so that they [might] turn from darkness to light and from the power of Satan to God" (Acts 26:18). And the apostles repeatedly warned Christians to "be sober-minded [and] watchful" because "your adversary the devil prowls around like a roaring lion, seeking someone to devour" (1 Peter 5:8). They did not want us to be either ignorant or underestimate Satan's strategies or power.

In our post-Enlightenment age, the very idea of a demon-haunted world is ridiculed. As Christians, this unbiblical naturalism can shape our assumptions and even cause us to feel embarrassed for holding a biblical, supernatural worldview many consider a foolish religious hangover from the Dark Ages.

But if we want to seriously engage in making "disciples of all nations" (Matt. 28:19) and see many "turn . . . from the power of Satan to God," we must be willing to endure the cultural shaming that comes from taking demons seriously. We must be more willing to be considered fools than cruelly leave people the victims of enslaving evil.

The more aligned we are with the Bible's view of reality, the more faithfully we will follow Jesus, the more spiritually helpful we will be to people, and the more damage we will wreak on the domain of darkness. But it also means we will bear the reproach Jesus endured (Heb. 13:13).

The Bible is a robustly supernatural book where God faithfully describes the spiritual war he's waging on the devil and his angels for the souls of fallen human beings. And his word to us through Paul is this:

> Be strong in the Lord and in the strength of his might. Put on the whole armor of God, that you may be able to stand against the schemes of the devil . . . and having done all, to stand firm. (Eph. 6:10–11, 13)

The war is real and dangerous. We must be aware of what hunts us, take them seriously, and not be ashamed that we do. And we must stand firm in the assault and determine not to leave people captive to demonic schemes. God will be faithful to give us the strength, courage, and spiritual weaponry we need.

MEDITATE MORE

Read Ephesians 6:13–17. When was the last time you seriously evaluated how well you're making use of the armor God has provided you?

26

So when the woman saw that the tree was good for food, and that it was a delight to the eyes, and that the tree was to be desired to make one wise, she took of its fruit and ate, and she also gave some to her husband who was with her, and he ate. GENESIS 3:6

Resist Temptation's Mirage Moment

GOD IS FAITHFUL ... TO REVEAL SATAN'S DECEPTIVE TACTICS

Temptation is not sin. We know this because Eve was tempted before she fell and Jesus was tempted, "yet without sin" (Heb. 4:15). Temptation is a disorienting, distorting experience when death is presented to us disguised as happiness. Sin occurs when we embrace the deception. One key to resisting temptation is learning to recognize what I call the "mirage moment."

A mirage is the hallucination that parched people sometimes experience in a hot desert. Their real thirst for water and the shimmering heat off the sand can deceive them into believing a refreshing oasis is in the distance, only to realize after they chase it that it wasn't real.

In temptation, the mirage moment occurs when a shimmering promise of increased joy or decreased misery appears where God says one doesn't exist. This deceptive mirage engages our emotions by tapping into our real thirst to be happy and presents us with a choice: Will we believe God's promise of happiness or the temptation's? At this point, we are tempted, but have not yet succumbed to sin.

The most notorious mirage moment occurred in Genesis 3. The satanic serpent appears in the garden, questions Eve about the forbidden tree, and then points her toward a shimmering promise of happiness where God said it doesn't exist:

"You will not surely die. For God knows that when you eat of it your eyes will be opened, and you will be like God, knowing good and evil" (Gen. 3:4–5).

What Eve saw was a rebellious mirage: "that the tree was good for food, and that it was a delight to the eyes, and that the tree was to be desired to make one wise" (Gen. 3:6). Satan tapped into Eve's God-given thirst to be happy and presented her with a choice: believe God's promise or the temptation's. When Eve *and Adam* decided to chase the mirage, it corrupted their desire, gave birth to sin, and brought forth death (James 1:14–15).

As we'll see in the next chapter, God faithfully sent his Son to redeem us by taking on himself the curse this rebellion (and ours) unleashed. But to save us from returning to sinful slavery, Jesus also faithfully gave us this warning: "Watch and pray that you may not enter into temptation" (Matt. 26:41), because Satan employs the same tactics with us. Jesus doesn't want us to be outwitted with shimmering false promises of happiness.

So, we must be *prayerfully watchful*. Expect Satan's mirage to be tempting. Our desire to be happy is God-given, so of course the mirage will promise us happiness, and threaten the loss of it if we resist. But remember, this mirage is death disguised as happiness. And remember, to be tempted is not a sin; to yield to it is sin. "Let not sin therefore reign in your mortal body, to make you obey its passions" (Rom. 6:12). Tempting mirages are never truly as strong as they feel.

And when they are presented, pray for help. For, as we'll see in the next few chapters, strong help is available to you and God will faithfully provide you a way of escape (1 Cor. 10:13).

PRAYER

Father, thank you for mercifully sending your Son to redeem me from the curse of my pursuits of rebellious, sinful mirages, and for faithfully revealing to me Satan's deceptive tactics. Give me grace today to be prayerfully watchful so that I am not deceived into believing any promise of happiness where you have said it doesn't exist. In Jesus' name, amen.

MEDITATE MORE

Read Genesis 3:1–6 and compare the mirage Satan presented to Eve with familiar mirages you find yourself drawn to believe. How would you put their false promises of happiness into words?

27

Then Jesus was led up by the Spirit into the wilderness to be tempted by the devil. MATTHEW 4:1

How Jesus Resisted Temptation

GOD IS FAITHFUL . . . TO GIVE YOU AN EXAMPLE TO FOLLOW

Scripture tells us that Jesus was tempted "in every respect . . . as we are, yet without sin," and therefore is "able to help those who are being tempted" (Heb. 4:15; 2:18). For the next few chapters, we'll explore various ways he faithfully helps us. We'll begin here by learning from the example he gave us when he was tempted at the start of his ministry.

Matthew 4:1–11 provides the most detailed account, recording three specific temptations and how Jesus resisted them with truth from Scripture. For the sake of space, I'll paraphrase the devil's tempting propositions, but I'll quote Jesus' responses in full.

> **Devil**: *You're hungry. If you're the Son of God, turn these stones to bread.*
> **Jesus**: "It is written, 'Man shall not live by bread alone, but by every word that comes from the mouth of God.'" (v. 4, quoting Deut. 8:3)

> **Devil**: *Scripture also says that angels will keep you from hurting a toe* (Ps. 91:11–12). *If you're the Son of God, jump off the temple and let's see.*
> **Jesus**: "Again it is written, 'You shall not put the Lord your God to the test.'" (v. 7, quoting Deut. 6:16)

> **Devil**: *See all these kingdoms? They're mine. But I'll give them to you if you'll worship me.*
> **Jesus**: "Be gone, Satan! For it is written, 'You shall worship the Lord your God and him only shall you serve.'" (v. 10, quoting Deut. 6:13)

What was the devil's strategy here? It's the same one he used on Adam and Eve. He got them to rebel against God by pitching them a different story than God had told them, an appealing but false story, and encouraged them to trust their perceptions more than God's promises. He was trying the same thing with Jesus.

In the first two temptations, the devil subtly proposed things that might at first appear innocuous. It's not sinful to eat when you're hungry, is it? And what would be sinful about the Son of God demonstrating his divine nature by miraculously making bread (as Jesus later did when he fed the five thousand)? Certainly, it's not sinful to trust a promise of Scripture! And wouldn't all Israel flock to you if credible witnesses see you falling and caught by angels?

When the subtle approach didn't work, the devil went for the jugular by appealing to Jesus' human fear of death and his divine dread of bearing the Father's wrath: *There is a way for you to have every knee bow and tongue confess your lordship that won't require your unspeakably horrible, sacrificial death: worship me.*

What was Jesus' strategy to resist these temptations? Keep the Father's Real Story in view. This is what his Scripture quotes reveal. He had come to "destroy the works of the devil" (1 John 3:8), undo the curse of the fall, and redeem his fallen people by doing what Adam and Eve had failed to do: faithfully trust his Father's promises over his human perceptions, since "whatever does not proceed from faith is sin" (Rom. 14:23).

Every temptation to sin is an appealing but false story about reality. But Jesus' example is one way he faithfully helps us resist. If we keep the Real Story in view when tempted and resolve to trust what God says over what we see, we are better able to see through the devil's deception and, like Jesus, remain "steadfast under trial" (James 1:12).

PRAYER

Father, thank you for the faithful example of your Son remaining steadfast when tempted. When I'm tempted to sin today, help me keep your Real Story in view so I can discern the emptiness and destructiveness of the devil's appealing lies. In Jesus' name, amen.

MEDITATE MORE

Read Genesis 3:1–7 and Matthew 4:1–11 and compare the devil's temptations. What appealing false stories are you vulnerable to believing?

28

Take care, brothers and sisters, that there will not be in any one of you an evil, unbelieving heart that falls away from the living God.

HEBREWS 3:12 NASB

How Jesus Helps You Fight Temptation (Part 1)

GOD IS FAITHFUL . . . TO REMIND YOU OF THE CONSEQUENCES OF UNBELIEF

In the previous chapter, we learned from Jesus' example how crucial it is to remember the Real Story we're in when facing temptation. This is because we respond to tempting desires or fears based on whatever story of reality we believe at the moment tells us will lead to more joy or less misery. If we believe a deceptive story, we will be "lured and enticed by [our] own desire," which when "conceived gives birth to sin, and [eventually] death" (James 1:14–15).

This is what makes the book of Hebrews so helpful. The author saw his original readers being enticed to abandon the great redemptive Story for a false one. So, he reminded them of the Real Story, but also reminded them of the consequences of unbelief. And in reminding them, he reminds us as well.

He reminds us how the exodus story foreshadowed the greater Story we're in—God is delivering his children from the horrible enslavement of sin through Jesus, a prophet greater than Moses (Heb. 3:3), who is faithfully guiding us to a better promised land, "that is, a heavenly one" (Heb. 11:16). He reminds us that Jesus is the prophesied priest-king after the order of Melchizedek (Heb. 7:17). And he reminds us that Jesus is a high priest greater than any of the countless high priests descended from Aaron (Heb. 7:23–25) who is mediating a better covenant than the old (Heb. 8:6), interceding for us in the holy place of "a greater and more perfect tent" (Heb. 9:11), having offered to God a better blood sacrifice than that of "goats and calves": "his own blood, thus securing an eternal redemption" (Heb. 9:12).

The author also reminds us of the grave consequences of sinful unbelief: how the generation of people who were delivered from Egypt "were unable to enter [the promised land] because of unbelief" (Heb. 3:19); how when it got hard they succumbed to the temptation to believe the whole escapade was a farce and the promise of some better land in the future by and by was a mirage of delusion, and they claimed "it would have been better for us to serve the Egyptians than to die in the wilderness" (Ex. 14:12); how as a result, that's exactly what happened—their "bodies fell in the wilderness" (Heb. 3:17). And therefore, he gives us this sober word: "Take care, brothers, lest there be in any of you an evil, unbelieving heart, leading you to fall away from the living God" (Heb. 3:12).

Through the author of Hebrews, God is faithful and loving to forthrightly warn us of the terrible consequences of succumbing to temptation. "While the promise of entering his rest still stands" (Heb. 4:1), he wants us to have a healthy fear lest any of us should fail to reach it, having been lured and enticed by "an evil, unbelieving heart." For our faithful, living God does not want us to fall away from him.

PRAYER

Father, thank you for so faithfully loving me that you're willing to give me fearful warnings of your judgment should I abandon the Real Story for a false, rebellious one. Give me grace to take your recommended care in guarding against an unbelieving heart by joining my brothers and sisters in receiving and giving needed exhortation, that none of us "may be hardened by the deceitfulness of sin" (Heb. 3:13). In Jesus' name, amen.

MEDITATE MORE

Read Hebrews 3–4 and receive whatever loving exhortation you discern from the Spirit.

| *For surely it is not angels that he helps, but he helps the offspring of Abraham.* HEBREWS 2:16

How Jesus Helps You
Fight Temptation (Part 2)

GOD IS FAITHFUL . . . TO MAKE YOU AN OFFSPRING OF ABRAHAM

You are a very experienced veteran of temptation. So am I. We've been tempted to sin every day of our lives since we were old enough to discern right from wrong. Given our experience, I'm sure you'll agree that we need all the help we can get to fight it.

The good news is that strong help is available: Jesus is a *mercifully eager* and *faithfully able* "high priest" who is "able to help those who are being tempted" (Heb. 2:17–18). But exactly how does he help us in the heat of a tempting moment? In this chapter and the following two, we'll examine three ways Jesus, in his role as our high priest, mercifully and faithfully helps us fight temptation, as explained in Hebrews 2:14–18.

> Since therefore the children share in flesh and blood, he himself likewise partook of the same things, that through death he might destroy the one who has the power of death, that is, the devil, and deliver all those who through fear of death were subject to lifelong slavery. For surely it is not angels that he helps, but he helps the offspring of Abraham. Therefore he had to be made like his brothers in every respect, so that he might become a merciful and faithful high priest in the service of God, to make propitiation for the sins of the people. For because he himself has suffered when tempted, he is able to help those who are being tempted.

Let's briefly focus here on how Jesus helps us by making us "offspring of Abraham" (v. 16).

The New Testament makes clear that the offspring of Abraham are not primarily his genetic offspring, but those "who [share] the faith of Abraham"

(Rom. 4:16). But this doesn't just happen. It required some very serious high priestly work on Jesus' part.

Jesus had to "be made like [us] in every respect" so he could (1) obey his Father perfectly on our behalf, and (2) offer himself as a "once for all" sacrifice (Heb. 7:27) to make "propitiation for [our] sins" (Heb. 2:17). In doing this, he broke "down in his flesh the dividing wall of hostility" between Jew and Gentile, "that he might create in himself one new man in place of the two" (Eph. 2:14–15). This means all the eternal covenant promises of God are included in the new covenant—the better covenant our high priest is mediating (Heb. 8:6)—and so apply to us. And this fulfilled God's promise to Abraham that in him "all the families of the earth shall be blessed" (Gen. 12:3).

What this means is that Jesus is faithfully able to help you because he mercifully has made you Abraham's offspring, allowing you to marshal all God's promises against temptation, since they all "find their Yes" for you in Jesus (2 Cor. 1:20).

PRAYER

Father, thank you for all you and your high priestly Son have mercifully and faithfully done to make me an offspring of Abraham, qualifying me "to share in the inheritance of the saints in light" (Col. 1:12), which includes receiving strong help when I'm tempted. In Jesus' name, amen.

MEDITATE MORE

Read Romans 4. Why is it important that being Abraham's offspring is based on faith rather than biology?

30

Since therefore the children share in flesh and blood, he himself likewise partook of the same things, that through death he might destroy the one who has the power of death, that is, the devil, and deliver all those who through fear of death were subject to lifelong slavery. HEBREWS 2:14–15

How Jesus Helps You Fight Temptation (Part 3)

GOD IS FAITHFUL ... TO LIBERATE YOU FROM THE FEAR OF DEATH

In the previous chapter, we saw how Jesus helps us fight temptation by making us "offspring of Abraham" (Heb. 2:16), thus making us beneficiaries of all God's covenant promises. As we make our way through Hebrews 2:14–18, we'll examine how our *mercifully eager* and *faithfully able* high priest helps us fight temptations that assault us through the "fear of death" (Heb. 2:15).

The fear of death is a gateway through which all manner of temptation enters to enslave us to sin. And this fear occurs on two levels.

The first level is our awareness of our *mortality*. We all fear death, and in the right measure, this isn't sinful. Our desire to live and not die is a God-given desire. Jesus experienced this desire "without sin" (Heb. 4:15). However, the devil knows how to magnify this fear into a tyrannical slave-master of temptation.

This side of the fall, the devil inverts the temptation he used with Adam and Eve. Now he tells us, "You shall not surely live. Eternal life is a delusion; your life is a vapor and that's all it is. So, you'd best grab as much life as you can while you have it. And if that's depressing—which it should be—why not just end your futile life right now?"

To the degree we believe him, we will waste inordinate amounts of time, energy, and money trying to postpone death as long as possible or seizing as many experiences and pleasures as possible for fear of missing out or distracting ourselves from the thought of death through all kinds of numbing entertainment and pursuits.

But Jesus is faithfully able to help us fight an enslaving fear of mortality by mercifully becoming for us "the resurrection and the life" and promising us abundant life beginning now and extending through eternity if we believe in him (John 11:25; 10:10; 3:16).

The second level of the fear of death is our awareness of our *sinfulness*. All of us, consciously or intuitively, know that after death "comes judgment" (Heb. 9:27) when "each of us will give an account of himself to God" (Rom. 14:12). The devil seeks to use this by tempting us with the fear of condemnation. He does his best to convince us that Jesus' atoning work will not save us from the guilt of our sin, so he can keep us enslaved to trying to achieve our own righteousness.

But Jesus is faithfully able to help us fight the fear of condemnation because he mercifully has taken away the guilt of our sin, which is the "sting of death," by fulfilling every "righteous requirement of the law" for us, so that through love, we can have "confidence for the day of judgment," thereby giving "us the victory" (1 Cor. 15:56–57; Rom. 8:4; 1 John 4:17).

Our high priest is mercifully eager and faithfully able to help us when we're tempted to believe death is the final end or that condemnation awaits us because he has accomplished everything necessary to deliver us from a lifelong enslavement to the fear of death.

PRAYER

Father, thank you for all you and your high priestly Son have mercifully and faithfully done to deliver me from a lifelong enslavement to the fear of death and provide me an escape from every tempting snare this fear lays for me. Deliver me from evil today by leading me out of any death-fear temptation. In Jesus' name, amen.

MEDITATE MORE

Read John 11:25–26. Do you believe this?

31

Therefore he had to be made like his brothers in every respect, so that he might become a merciful and faithful high priest in the service of God, to make propitiation for the sins of the people. For because he himself has suffered when tempted, he is able to help those who are being tempted. HEBREWS 2:17-18

How Jesus Helps You Fight Temptation (Part 4)

GOD IS FAITHFUL . . . TO GIVE YOU A HIGH PRIEST WHO SYMPATHIZES WITH YOU

In the previous two chapters, we've seen from Hebrews 2:14–18 how Jesus, our high priest, is mercifully eager and faithfully able to help us in temptation by making us offspring of Abraham, qualifying us to share in all of God's covenant promises, and freeing us from the tyranny of the lifelong fear of death. Here we'll examine how because Jesus "himself has suffered when tempted, he is able to help those who are being tempted" (Heb. 2:17–18).

First, what suffering of Jesus is the author of Hebrews referring to? Almost certainly, he had the suffering Jesus experienced in Gethsemane through the crucifixion primarily in mind. But I doubt that's all he had in mind. In chapter 4, he tells us that Jesus was tempted "in every respect . . . as we are, yet without sin" (Heb. 4:15). If "righteous Lot . . . was tormenting his righteous soul over [the] lawless deeds that he saw and heard" in Sodom (2 Peter 2:7–8), we can only imagine what it was like for the sinless Son of God to live in this sin-saturated world.

So, how does Jesus' suffering in temptation help us? It means that he is mercifully able to "sympathize with our weaknesses" (Heb. 4:15). Jesus knows what temptation is like from experience—temptation more intense and agonizing than we likely will ever know. And since "he always lives to make intercession" for us with the Father, he is able to faithfully provide us "the way of escape" for each temptation we face, so we can faithfully endure it (Heb. 7:25; 1 Cor. 10:13).

This is the good news we have when facing temptation: strong help is available! Jesus, our great high priest, is *eager to help us* because he's merciful and sympathetic, and he's *able to help us* because he's faithful in his service to God on our behalf.

But not only this. When we fail and succumb to sin's temptation—because of the whole scope of Jesus' high priestly ministry—"if we confess our sins, he is [faithfully able] and just to [mercifully] forgive us our sins and to cleanse us from all unrighteousness," which he is also eager to do (1 John 1:9).

When we're tempted today, "Let us . . . with confidence draw near to the throne of grace, that we may receive mercy and find grace to help in time of need" (Heb. 4:16). Because our high priest, who has made us offspring of Abraham, delivered us from the fear of death, and has himself suffered when tempted, is *mercifully eager* and *faithfully able* to help us in every temptation. And should we fail and sin, we don't need to wallow in condemnation (Rom. 8:1–2), for he has also made it possible for the Father to be faithful and just to forgive us. We only need to confess our sin, receive our promised forgiveness, then get back up and back in the fight.

PRAYER

Father, thank you for all you and your high priestly Son have mercifully and faithfully done to make it possible for Jesus to sympathize with my weaknesses and effectively intercede for me so that I have a way of escape with every temptation. Help me discern those escape-ways in whatever temptations I face today so I can faithfully endure it. In Jesus' name, amen.

MEDITATE MORE

Read Hebrews 4:14–16.

32

Take care, brothers and sisters, that there will not be in any one of you an evil, unbelieving heart that falls away from the living God. But encourage one another every day, as long as it is still called "today," so that none of you will be hardened by the deceitfulness of sin. HEBREWS 3:12–13 NASB

Don't Let Your Resistance Rob You of God's Grace

GOD IS FAITHFUL . . . NOT TO LEAVE YOU TO FIGHT UNBELIEF ALONE

This text is a very sober warning of the danger unbelief is to us. We need wise brothers and sisters—those who know how to care for vulnerable souls—to help us discern what's true when sinful desires, faithless fears, the anxiety of doubt, and the darkness of despair get a hold on us and distort our perceptions of reality.

But here's why we need such a strong exhortation: when our perceptions are distorted is often when we least want to expose what's going on inside. Sin's promise appears very alluring; the threats of fear and doubt feel terrifying and seem inescapable. So, when our need is most acute, we feel the most acute internal resistance to pursuing it or receiving it.

Why do we feel such resistance to pursuing or receiving help when we need it most? Three common contributors are *pride* (my perception of what's true is more trustworthy than I believe yours will be), *shame* (I don't want you to see my evil or weakness), and *fear* (you may reject me, or harm me).

The sin of pride always leads us toward destruction (Prov. 16:18). But shame and fear are usually complex emotions, fueled partly by sinful tendencies in us and partly by experiences that make us guarded, such as damage we've suffered in a painful past. The net effect is that these responses distort how we view those who might help us, undermining our trust in them and instead producing resistance toward them.

The danger of this resistance is that it leads to confusing, dangerous places. Sinful desires, misplaced fears, doubt, and despair undermine our trust in what God has promised us in his word and our trust in our brothers and sisters. Unbelief can become a vicious cycle, leaving us isolated and increasingly vulnerable to more deception. The Bible's warnings about this are clear:

> Whoever isolates himself seeks his own desire; he breaks out against all sound judgment. (Prov. 18:1)

> Whoever trusts in his own mind is a fool, but he who walks in wisdom will be delivered. (Prov. 28:26)

In the dangerous, distrustful days of the Third Reich's reign of terror, Dietrich Bonhoeffer wrote to his fraternal Christian community: "A Christian needs another Christian who speaks God's Word to him. He needs him again and again when he becomes uncertain and discouraged, for by himself he cannot help himself without belying the truth."[15]

This is true. We need this more than we know—*especially* when evil unbelief has infected us, and we feel strong internal resistance to sharing it with another trustworthy Christian.

Trusting in the Lord with all our heart is a community project. This is why the Lord requires us to humble ourselves and confide our sinful desires, faithless fears, anxious doubts, and despairing thoughts in trusted members of the faith community the Lord faithfully provides for us—and distrust our resistance to do so, because he has ordained that we receive the Spirit's help through them. For it's when we're on our own that we are most likely to be hardened by the deceitfulness of sin.

PRAYER

Father, thank you for this sober scriptural warning and for the faithful provision of my brothers and sisters so that I have the help I need to fight unbelief. Give me the discernment I need to recognize when faithless resistance rises up in me and the grace to distrust it, so I don't forgo the grace you wish to give me through others. In Jesus' name, amen.

MEDITATE MORE

Read Hebrews 3–4:2. What's the connection between the exhortation in Hebrews 3:13 and the context of the failure of the Israelites "whose bodies fell in the wilderness" (Heb. 3:17)?

33

Look carefully then how you walk, not as unwise but as wise, making the best use of the time, because the days are evil.

EPHESIANS 5:15–16

Just Enough Time

GOD IS FAITHFUL . . . TO GIVE YOU JUST ENOUGH TIME TO DO HIS WILL

I don't have enough time." How often have you said this? I've said it countless times, and probably thought it countless more times. But have you ever considered how dishonoring this claim is to God? It essentially says God is either negligent or stingy in providing us time. This freshly struck me when I heard Prof. Bruce Hindmarsh say,

> Busyness is moral laziness. . . . God has given us just enough time to do what we need to do moment by moment to respond to him. And his grace is there; it is eternally present. Every moment is a sacrament where time touches eternity, and there is exactly enough time to do what God has called us to do.[16]

Moral laziness? How is being very busy morally lazy? Prof. Hindmarsh identifies three reasons. One is that busyness is a way of telling *ourselves* and—perhaps more importantly—*others* how essential we are—a way of posturing our significance. A second reason is that busyness provides a convenient escape from taking responsibility for making a difficult, complex decision; we'd rather be the victim of circumstances than be responsible for a mistake. My colleague, Tony Reinke calls this "lazy busy."[17] A third reason is that an overflowing schedule can shield us from the unpredictable, inconvenient, time-consuming needs of other people. Who can accuse you of not loving someone if you're simply swamped? Well, God can (1 John 3:16–18).

The truth is, God is neither negligent nor stingy in his provision of time. "Every moment is a sacrament where time touches eternity, and there is exactly enough time to do what God has called us to do." He has uniquely created each of us with our strengths and weaknesses, and he's given each of us unique callings and unique responsibilities for which he will hold us uniquely accountable (Matt. 25:14–30; 2 Cor. 5:10).

It is hard work to develop the discipline of looking carefully how we walk, "not as unwise but as wise, making the best use of the time" God provides us. That's what makes busyness a moral and faith issue. If, like Moses in Exodus 18, our God-given responsibilities are wearing us out, we may need to seek out a "Jethro" to help us find a wiser approach (see chapter 51). But if our busyness is due to the kinds of morally lazy motivations Prof. Hindmarsh described, it is a weighty sin God wants us to lay aside so we can run the race God has given us with faithful endurance (Heb. 12:1).

Either way, we must not dishonor God by claiming we don't have enough time. God may, and frequently does, fill our time-plates full, but his sufficient grace is here, right now, in the sacred gift of this moment, where time touches eternity. As we prayerfully trust him, he will faithfully give us "just enough time to do what we need to do moment by moment to respond to him."

PRAYER

Father, thank you for faithfully providing me just enough time to do what you've given me to do. Forgive me for all the times I've called that into question by claiming not to have enough time, and for all the times I've been unfaithfully busy due to my moral laziness. Give me sufficient grace in every sacred moment today to walk carefully in wisdom and make the best use of the time you give me. In Jesus' name, amen.

MEDITATE MORE

Read Ephesians 5:1–21. What does Paul mean by "making the best use of the time"?

34

"Come to me, all who labor and are heavy laden, and I will give you rest. Take my yoke upon you, and learn from me, for I am gentle and lowly in heart, and you will find rest for your souls. For my yoke is easy, and my burden is light." MATTHEW 11:28-30

Come to Jesus for Rest

GOD IS FAITHFUL . . . TO GIVE YOU THE REST YOU NEED MOST

Life is hard. So much can make us feel weary: our vocational labors, our parenting labors, our ministry labors, our relational conflicts, our sudden or chronic illnesses. Almost everything we do can at times exhaust us. But what makes us most weary aren't the things we *do*; it's what we *believe*.

Our beliefs either lighten our burdens or add to them. Jesus knew this. That's why at times he would look out on the crowd of people flocking to him, and he'd overflow with compassion "because they were harassed and helpless, like sheep without a shepherd" (Matt. 9:36). And because of his great compassion, we have one of the most beautiful gospel invitations from God to sinners in all of Scripture: "Come to me, all who labor and are heavy laden, and I will give you rest."

That is what we deeply long for: *rest for our souls*. For the hardest burdens to bear are our soul burdens. And so often what burdens our souls are the effects of false beliefs—lies we believe about God, ourselves, others, the world, the future, and life that weigh down our hearts with sorrow, fear, anxiety, discouragement, or despair.

The degree that something we believe drains us of hope is the degree to which that belief burdens our souls. For our souls only find peace and rest in hope. This is why we find Scripture recording God's people saying things like, "Why are you cast down, O my soul, and why are you in turmoil within me? Hope in God" (Ps. 42:11).

Hope is what we're frantically looking for whenever our souls are heavy laden. But hope is only as good as what it rests on is true. A false hope will eventually become its own unbearable soul-burden.

And that is why Jesus cried out, "Come to me!" The God of hope himself—our compassionate Shepherd who wishes to bear our sin, "daily [bear] our burden" (Ps. 68:19 NASB), guide us through danger to places of refreshment (Ps. 23:1–4), provide us all we need (Phil. 4:19), and bring us "safely into his heavenly kingdom" (2 Tim. 4:18)—this God invites us to come to him and receive from him rest for our souls.

Yes, he invites *us*. Jesus feels the same compassion toward us when we're heavy-laden as he did to the weary, harassed people he addressed that day. And he extends his invitation as urgently and tenderly to us as he did them. His great desire is that we find the rest we so desperately need, the rest that only he can give.

So, come to him today, "casting all your anxieties on him, because he cares for you" (1 Peter 5:7). And if you do, the faithful "God of hope [will] fill you with all joy and peace in believing, so that by the power of the Holy Spirit you may abound in hope" (Rom. 15:13).

PRAYER

Father, thank you for offering to me, through your glorious Son, the invitation for me to come and receive rest for my soul—the rest I most need. Help me today to discern and refuse every lie that will rob me of this rest and choose rather to "live by faith in the Son of God, who loved me and gave himself for me" (Gal. 2:20)—the rest only he can give. In Jesus' name, amen.

MEDITATE MORE

Read Luke 12:22–34, where Jesus gives one picture of what living in his soul-rest looks like.

35

"Take my yoke upon you, and learn from me, for I am gentle and lowly in heart, and you will find rest for your souls. For my yoke is easy, and my burden is light." MATTHEW 11:29–30

What Makes Jesus' Yoke Easy

GOD IS FAITHFUL . . . TO BEAR YOUR HEAVIEST YOKE AND LIGHTEN YOUR EVERY BURDEN

What precisely is this easy yoke Jesus offers us? Jesus provided an answer to this question when someone asked him, "What must we do, to be doing the works of God?" "This is the work of God," he responded, "that you believe in him whom he has sent" (John 6:28–29). The easy yoke Jesus offers us is simply to trust him.

And in exchange, Jesus mercifully and faithfully removes our inconceivably and unbearably heavy yoke of sin's condemnation and penalty and places it on his own shoulders. In bearing "our sins in his body on the tree" (1 Peter 2:24) he purchased not only our justification (2 Cor. 5:21), but also the fulfillment of every promise that makes it possible for him to give us the soul-rest we so desperately need.

"Come, take my easy yoke . . . and my light burden." My goodness, who would not want to receive such a wonderful invitation?

But one thing we must keep in mind is that in offering us his easy yoke and light burden, Jesus isn't offering us an easy, burdenless life in this age. He's not implying that our vocational, parenting, and ministry labors, our relational conflicts, illnesses, persecutions, spiritual warfare, and many other struggles and suffering will no longer weary us. For Jesus did say, "The way is hard that leads to life" (Matt. 7:14).

In fact, in another great invitation, Jesus said, "If anyone would come after me, let him deny himself and take up his cross daily and follow me" (Luke 9:23). This sounds very different from his offer to give us an easy yoke, light burden, and soul-rest. Is Jesus calling us to a life of refreshing rest, or to a life of sacrificial dying?

The answer, as you might expect, is both. These invitations aren't contradictory, they're complementary. Accepting Jesus' invitation to receive rest for our souls is what makes it possible to accept his invitation to follow him on the hard Calvary road. For when our soul has been relieved of its unbearable yoke, and when "the God of hope [fills us] with all joy and peace in believing, so that by the power of the Holy Spirit [we] may abound in hope" (Rom. 15:13), we are able to view adversity and suffering on the hard way leading to life as "light momentary affliction . . . preparing for us an eternal weight of glory beyond all comparison" (2 Cor. 4:17).

Coming to Jesus for rest doesn't shield us from afflictions. It transforms afflictions from fear-dominating, anxiety-producing, and hopeless to "light" and "momentary." Hoping in the God of hope makes all the difference.

So, Jesus says to us, "Come to me . . . and you will find rest for your souls." And when we do, he is faithful to make good on his promise. And because he does, he is able to say to us, "In the world you will have tribulation. But take heart; I have overcome the world" (John 16:33).

PRAYER

Father, thank you for all that you and your faithful Son have done to give me the inexpressibly wonderful gift of removing my unbearable yoke and receive Jesus' easy one, which also now makes every other affliction I'll ever bear in this age "light" and "momentary" in comparison to the eternal life you have in store for me. In Jesus' name, amen.

MEDITATE MORE

Read 2 Corinthians 4:7–18 and reflect on how Jesus' easy yoke made Paul's significant afflictions "light" and "momentary" for him.

36

*To keep me from becoming conceited because of the surpassing
greatness of the revelations, a thorn was given me in the flesh.*

2 CORINTHIANS 12:7

Why You Have That Thorn

GOD IS FAITHFUL . . . TO GIVE YOU THE THORN YOU NEED

I have a "thorn in the flesh." It weakens me, making nearly everything I do harder. I have pleaded with God, sometimes in tears, for it to be removed. But it remains. You likely have your own thorn, or you will at some point. Yours will be different from mine, but its purpose will be similar. For we are given thorns that weaken us in order to make us stronger.

The term "thorn in the flesh" comes from the verse above. Paul's "thorn" is among the most famous afflictions in history, and we don't even know what it was. There are a number of plausible possibilities: a chronic physical condition such as the eye malady he referred to in Galatians 4:13, 15; spiritual-psychological struggles from the cumulative trauma he endured (2 Cor. 11); the false "super-apostles" wreaking havoc in the churches he planted (2 Cor. 11:5, 26); or something else altogether.

The fact that we don't know what Paul's thorn was turns out to be both merciful and instructive to us. It's merciful because it allows us all in our afflictions to identify with Paul to some degree. It's instructive because God's purpose for Paul's mysterious thorn was similar to God's purpose for ours.

Paul said God gave him his thorn to keep him from "becoming conceited." Pride, in all its manifestations, is our most pervasive and most dangerous sin. Therefore, whatever God gives us to keep us humble and prayerfully dependent on him is a great gift—even when that gift causes us pain. Which means, if God faithfully afflicts us in order to protect us from joy-destroying pride, it's a great kindness. Redemptive pain can protect us from destructive pain.

Like Paul's, our thorns weaken us. Sometimes they're visible to others, but often they're hidden from public view, known only to a few. Thorns are never romantic, never heroic. Rather, along with making life harder, they tend to humble us in unflattering ways that detract from rather than enhance our reputations.

But this is the way our thorns have to be. Because if they were noble and heroic, they would be of no help in guarding us from our pervasive pride. That's why, as with Paul, God often answers our pleas for deliverance with a no. Because without the thorn, we would never experience that God's "grace is sufficient" for us, that his "power is made perfect in weakness" (2 Cor. 12:9).

This is why we have our thorns. They are weakeners that strengthen us. Without them, we would choose a weaker strength and miss experiencing the glory and joy of God's powerful, faithful, sufficient grace. It's another wonderful kingdom paradox: our agonizing thorns end up producing greater joy in us and ultimately make us more effective and fruitful. The more we press into this paradox, the more we will say with Paul, "For the sake of Christ, then, I am content with weaknesses, insults, hardships, persecutions, and calamities. For when I am weak, then I am strong" (2 Cor. 12:10).

PRAYER

Father, thank you for every great gift you've ever given to me to humble me and make me prayerfully dependent on you—even if that's been a persistent and painful thorn in the flesh. You are faithful and kind in all your ways. Give me your sufficient grace today to be content with the strengthening weakness you've granted me. In Jesus' name, amen.

MEDITATE MORE

Read 2 Corinthians 12:7–10. When was the last time you were able to say with joyful faith, "When I am weak, then I am strong"?

37

To keep me from becoming conceited because of the surpassing greatness of the revelations, a thorn was given me in the flesh, a messenger of Satan to harass me, to keep me from becoming conceited. 2 CORINTHIANS 12:7

When Satan Pierces You with a Thorn from God

GOD IS FAITHFUL . . . TO USE SATANIC THORNS FOR YOUR GOOD

In this one sentence, Paul makes two amazing, yet potentially disturbing, statements about his painful thorn. The first is that *God gave him his thorn.* It's clear from the context that Paul identified God as his thorn-giver, not Satan. And he understood that God's purpose was to keep him humble and dependent on Christ's power (2 Cor. 12:9).

But the second statement is more shocking. Paul says God gave him his thorn *through "a messenger of Satan."* Suddenly, we find ourselves in an even deeper part of the theological pool. And given the ease with which Paul says this, he clearly expects us to be able to swim here.

Can Satan pierce us with a thorn from God? Yes. Does this trouble us? Does it trouble us that it didn't trouble Paul? Notice that Paul feels no need to qualify or explain how God can lovingly and faithfully give his child a redemptive gift of pain through an evil means. Why? Because Paul knows his Old Testament like the back of his hand, and this phenomenon is woven right through it.

There was Joseph who, looking back on his brothers' evil motives for selling him into slavery—not to mention Potiphar's wife's evil actions that unjustly landed him in an Egyptian prison—was able to say to them, "As for you, you meant evil against me, but God meant it for good, to bring it about that many people should be kept alive, as they are today" (Gen. 50:20).

There was David who often felt that there was "but a step between me and death" (1 Sam. 20:3) as Saul, tormented by "a harmful spirit from God" (1 Sam. 18:10), repeatedly tried to assassinate him. Yet the result was that David became a king who was able to say, "Into your hand I commit my spirit; you have redeemed me, O LORD, faithful God" (Ps. 31:5).

There was Daniel, whose envious palace adversaries concocted an evil plot to trap him into a death sentence. Yet what it ended up producing was King Darius's confession to the world that "the God of Daniel . . . is the living God, enduring forever; his kingdom shall never be destroyed, and his dominion shall be to the end" (Dan. 6:26).

And there was Jesus, who was "delivered up according to the definite plan and foreknowledge of God" to be "crucified and killed by the hands of lawless men" (Acts 2:23) so that "whoever believes in him should not perish but have eternal life" (John 3:16).

Our redemptive thorns also may be delivered by a satanic messenger. But God is so powerful, so wise, and so faithful that he can work all things—including our demonically induced afflictions—for our everlasting good (Rom. 8:28). They become more ways that God "disarm[s] the rulers and authorities and put[s] them to open shame" (Col. 2:15). Therefore, when they come, we can, with Paul, "boast all the more gladly of [our] weaknesses, so that the power of Christ may rest upon [us]" (2 Cor. 12:9).

PRAYER

Father, I marvel at such sovereign power, wisdom, and faithfulness that allows you to even make messengers of Satan become means of delivering your children good, redemptive gifts. As you did for Paul, give me sufficient grace to discern when you are using an evil means to make your Son's power perfect in my weakness so I can gladly boast in his power. In Jesus' name, amen.

MEDITATE MORE

Read 2 Corinthians 12:7–10 (*again* if you read this after the previous meditation). When was the last time you sincerely felt like boasting in Christ's power being displayed through a weakness you experience?

Are You Investing Your Weaknesses Well?

GOD IS FAITHFUL . . . TO GIVE YOU THE WEAKNESSES YOU NEED

How well are you investing the weaknesses you've been given? Has anyone ever asked you that question before? It sounds strange, I know. After all, people invest assets in order to increase their value. They don't invest liabilities. They try to eliminate or minimize liabilities. It's easy for us to see our strengths as assets. But most of us naturally consider our weaknesses as liabilities—deficiencies to eliminate or minimize.

But God entrusts to us our weaknesses just as he does our strengths. In God's economy, where the return on investment he most values is "love that issues from a pure heart and a good conscience and a sincere faith" (1 Tim. 1:5), weaknesses become assets—we could even call them talents—to be stewarded, to be invested. It may even be that the most valuable asset God has given you to steward is not a strength, but a weakness.

You might recognize that I'm drawing imagery from Jesus' parable of the talents (Matt. 25:14–30). In Jesus' day, talents were monetary units of immense value. Jesus has given each of us "talents" to steward, "each according to his ability" (Matt. 25:15). His expectation is that we will invest them well while we wait for his return.

Some of these talents are strengths and abilities our Lord has given us. But some of them are our weaknesses, inadequacies, and limitations, which he's also given to us. And he's given us these weaknesses not only to increase in us the invaluable and shareable treasure of humility (2 Cor. 12:7), but also to increase our strength in the most important aspects of our being: faith in God and love for God and others (2 Cor. 12:10).

But our weaknesses are not only given to us as individuals; they are also given to the church. Our limitations, as much as our abilities, are crucial to

Christ's design to equip his body so that it works properly and "builds itself up in love" (Eph. 4:16). Our weaknesses make us depend on one another in ways our strengths don't (1 Cor. 12:21–26). Which means they are given to the church for the same reason they are given to us individually: so that the church may grow strong in faith (1 Cor. 2:3–5) and love (1 Cor. 13)—two qualities that uniquely manifest Jesus' reality and power to the world (John 13:35).

Someday, when our Master returns, he will ask us to give an account of the talents he's entrusted to us. Some of those talents will be our weaknesses. We don't want to tell him we buried any of them. We may discover that the most valuable talent in our investment portfolio was actually a weakness.

Since "it is required of stewards that they be found faithful" (1 Cor. 4:2), we would be wise to examine how faithfully we are stewarding the talents of our weaknesses. So, how well are you investing the weaknesses you've been given?

PRAYER

Father, thank you for faithfully entrusting to me my weaknesses, just as you have my strengths, and forgive me for any ways I have neglected to value them as you do. Give me grace to faithfully steward both my strengths and weaknesses today. In Jesus' name, amen.

MEDITATE MORE

Read Matthew 25:14–30, and when Jesus refers to "talents," think of some of the weaknesses God has entrusted to you.

> *For as in one body we have many members, and the members do not all have the same function, so we, though many, are one body in Christ, and individually members one of another.* ROMANS 12:4–5

One Body and Individual Members of One Another

GOD IS FAITHFUL ... TO EMPOWER HIS WHOLE CHURCH

This description of the church as a body is more than simply an analogy; it is the revealing of a mystery. The church isn't fundamentally an organization; it's fundamentally an organism. Christ's body is alive. And like a human body, it is an incarnation of unity in diversity.

A body is a singular unit created by God to do certain things. The individual members on their own cannot fulfill all the purposes for which the body was created. Those members must function together as a collective whole in order for the body to do all it was created to do.

But the church is also "many members." There is no collective body without its countless crucial individual members. God's faithful and glorious design of the body of Christ, like a human body, is a large-scale interdependency of diverse members functioning in complementary roles to make it possible for the body to function. This way God bestows profound dignity and honor upon both the collective whole and the individual members.

But this design means different members will be compelled to do different things. Some will discern an urgent need to counter false teaching in the church, and others an urgent need to care for people in need, others an urgent need to end some social evil, others an urgent need to create more effective administrative structures to better serve the collective whole, others an urgent need to address painful racial divisions, and others an urgent need to give themselves to intercession and prayer ministry.

This design requires humility and faith in each member. All these things (and many more) matter greatly, and our great Head cares passionately about them all. But no individual can give themselves to addressing all these needs. The Spirit empowers each of us to perform limited roles for "the common good" (1 Cor. 12:7). Our roles might change in different seasons of our lives, but in whatever role we currently find ourselves, we must not pridefully assume others should feel our level of urgency over a need we're assigned to address. Likewise, we should not pridefully assume roles the Spirit hasn't empowered us to perform. We must prayerfully trust our body's faithful Head and Spirit to provide what is needed for the common good at the times and places they deem best.

Understanding that we "are one body . . . and individually members one of another" is a wonderful, liberating gift from our faithful Creator. It frees us from feeling obligated to perform functions in the body for which we aren't equipped so we can focus on the indispensable function for which the Spirit has equipped us for the sake of the common good. And it frees us to be grateful to God for his incredible grace toward us all, and grateful for the indispensable gifts others are to the body.

Therefore, "as each has received a gift, use it to serve one another, as good stewards of God's varied grace . . . in order that in everything God may be glorified through Jesus Christ" (1 Peter 4:10–11).

PRAYER

Father, your design of the body of Christ is marvelous and magnificent. Your faithfulness to each member and the collective whole is evident. Give me grace today to faithfully perform the function for which I've been equipped and also give me eyes to see more clearly how much the body benefits from your equipping others for their callings so I will grow in gratitude for them. May you be glorified through Jesus in my church today. Amen.

MEDITATE MORE

Read 1 Peter 4:7–11.

40 | *But as it is, God arranged the members in the body, each one of them, as he chose.* 1 CORINTHIANS 12:18

You Are Indispensable

GOD IS FAITHFUL . . . IN ASSIGNING YOU YOUR ROLE IN CHRIST'S BODY

The way God designed your human body is pure genius. It is unity in diversity incarnate. You comprise an almost incomprehensible number of unique parts that all function together, and each part, strong or weak, prominent or obscure, is necessary to make it possible for you to do what you do every day. So it is with the body of Christ. It is marvelous and magnificent, comprising an almost incomprehensible number of unique members, each of which, strong or weak, prominent or obscure, is necessary precisely because of his or her unique, God-assigned role.

Let's make it personal: *you* are necessary precisely because of your unique, God-assigned role. I wonder if you believe that.

Most of us can see how the entire church, the collective body, is necessary to God's purposes in the world. And most of us can see how particular members of the body are necessary. But it's easy to doubt that *all* the members, particularly ourselves, are really necessary. That's why the Spirit, through Paul, felt it necessary to address our doubts:

> If the foot should say, "Because I am not a hand, I do not belong to the body," that would not make it any less a part of the body. And if the ear should say, "Because I am not an eye, I do not belong to the body," that would not make it any less a part of the body. (1 Cor. 12:15–16)

In other words, when we judge ourselves or anyone else as unimportant to Christ's body, we cannot trust our assessment:

The eye cannot say to the hand, "I have no need of you," nor again the head to the feet, "I have no need of you." On the contrary, the parts of the body that seem to be weaker are indispensable. (1 Cor. 12:21–22)

Indispensable is a strong term, and it applies to you. *You* are indispensable, not because you feel indispensable, not because others tell you you're indispensable, but because God chose you: "God arranged the members in the body, each one of them, as he chose." God himself has assigned you a role in the well-being and function of Christ's body. And he has given you a "manifestation of the Spirit for the common good" (1 Cor. 12:7).

The way God designed the body of Christ is pure genius. And he has made each member necessary to what the church is called to do today. When it comes to assessing your relative importance to the body of Christ, don't lean on your own understanding. Trust your faithful Head's assessment because he knows better than you do. Nor is it your responsibility to make that assessment—it's Jesus' responsibility. And his assessment is, "I have need of you." Your responsibility, along with your brothers and sisters in the body, is to use whatever gift you've received from the Spirit to faithfully serve others "as good stewards of God's varied grace . . . in order that in everything God may be glorified through Jesus Christ" (1 Peter 4:10–11).

PRAYER

Father, thank you for making every member of Christ's body, strong or weak, prominent or obscure, indispensable for the functioning of his body today. Forgive me for every time I have wrongly assessed any member's indispensability, including my own. Help me discern and steward well any gifts you've given me for the common good of your people, that you may be glorified through your Son, in whose name I pray, amen.

MEDITATE MORE

Read 1 Corinthians 12:1–27.

41

> *For just as the body is one and has many members, and all the members of the body, though many, are one body, so it is with Christ.* 1 CORINTHIANS 12:12

When You Discover Your Indispensable Role

GOD IS FAITHFUL . . . TO SHOW YOU WHY HE CREATED YOU

Imagine you've agreed to participate in an experiment where you're asked to identify whatever is placed before you. You don't know it, but you're about to view anatomical parts of a largemouth bass. First comes the translucent green pectoral fin. You look at it and guess, "Is it some kind of leaf?" Next comes the slimy swim bladder. "Gross! Is it some small animal's intestine?" Next comes a red piece of gill tissue. "I have no idea what that is!"

Had you viewed these parts in the context of the fish's body, you'd grasp to some degree their importance in helping the fish function properly. But taken out of the context of the body, the parts make little sense. "So it is with Christ." Each of us is a part of the body of Christ and has a particular function. But it takes the body of Christ to understand the function of a part and it takes all the parts to make the body function.

If you're struggling to figure out what part of Christ's body you are, one possibility is that you're examining yourself out of context. This is understandable, since our culture teaches us to see ourselves as autonomous individuals rather than interdependent parts of a larger social organism. But here's the problem: we aren't designed to be independent bodies primarily doing our own thing. God designed us as interdependent body parts that contribute to the healthy functioning of a larger social body. So, if we structure our lives primarily as autonomous individuals, we'll find discerning our role in Christ's body elusive and perplexing.

We aren't each individual "bodies" of Christ. We collectively "are the body of Christ and individually members of it" (1 Cor. 12:27). Our lives are meant to make sense in the context of Christ's body because each of us has a God-given function to perform—a function that is interdependent with other functioning parts.

Christ's body—and what Paul primarily has in mind in 1 Corinthians 12 is the local church—is the primary context in which God intends for our unique spiritual gifts and kingdom callings to be revealed, confirmed, and engaged.

Millennia before there were tests for profiling our personalities, finding our strengths, or identifying our spiritual gifts, there was the local church, where each member was "given the manifestation of the Spirit for the common good" (1 Cor. 12:7). That's what your spiritual gifts are for: the common good of your local church.

Of course, no church does "body life" perfectly because they're all made up of imperfect people, like us. And sometimes a local "body" is so diseased that God may direct us to find a healthier body. But nonetheless, the local church is God's corporeal provision for us, the context where our lives are meant to make sense.

So, how do you discover your role in your local expression of Christ's body? There's no one formula, no quick test. It happens in the messiness of body life. But if you fixate less on your particular part and more on the good of others and the common good of the larger body, God will faithfully show you what member you are. That's God's design. "Pursue love" (1 Cor. 14:1), and you will discover his will for you. Seek first the kingdom, and all you need will be provided (Matt. 6:33).

PRAYER

Father, thank you again for the way you've designed the body of Christ and my role in it. And thank you for my local church. Teach me to increasingly see myself as an interdependent part you've equipped to contribute to the healthy functioning of the body in which you've placed me. In Jesus' name, amen.

MEDITATE MORE

Read Romans 12:3–8.

42

The eye cannot say to the hand, "I have no need of you," nor again the head to the feet, "I have no need of you." On the contrary, the parts of the body that seem to be weaker are indispensable.

1 CORINTHIANS 12:21–22

You Are So Limited Because You're So Loved

GOD IS FAITHFUL . . . IN CREATING YOU WITH ALL YOUR LIMITATIONS

This text reveals something glorious about God's design of the whole body of Christ and your particular role: God created you to be so limited because he loves you. If you don't feel loved because of your limitations, perhaps you're looking from the wrong perspective.

What do our limitations have to do with love? The reasons are too vast to recount here. But I'll focus on this one: God made us to experience love most in the places where grace is most needed. This is true both in how we receive love (from God and others), and in how we give love.

When it comes to God, the more we grasp his incomprehensible love for us in all he's done to graciously meet our immeasurable need (Eph. 3:19), the greater our love for him grows. That's why the woman forgiven by Jesus of her great sins had the greater love for God than Simon the Pharisee (Luke 7:47). Our greatest experience of God's love for us is in the place of our greatest need for his grace.

It's also true that we experience the most love for one another in the places of our greatest mutual needs. When God gave us our strengths, his purpose was so we could have the astounding privilege of loving someone else by graciously serving them in a place of their need and receive their grateful love in return. Conversely, when God gave us our weaknesses, his purpose was so we could have the astounding privilege of humbly receiving someone else's love as they graciously serve us in a place of our need and joyfully responding to them with grateful love in return.

And just like the vertical reverberation of love between God and us, there are horizontal reverberations of love between us as we extend love to one another. And since God is love and all love originates in him (1 John 4:7–8), the vertical and horizontal reverberations all meld together into one glorious praise song of love to God.

Do you see God's beautiful design of love in our limitations? The transactions of love occur in the very places of our various and different needs.

God has given you so many limitations because he loves you. He wants you to experience as much of his love, in as many ways as possible. And for that to happen, he must provide you a never-ending river of reasons and an enormous range of diverse ways to receive and give love.

And this is just what he's done! He has made you a very limited part of his body, the church, and he places you with other parts that are also very limited in different ways (1 Cor. 12:18, 27). As the interdependent parts work together, the whole body functions (Rom. 12:4–5), and it displays the love of God (John 13:34–35). Both your unique, limited strengths and weaknesses are indispensable gifts to Christ's body, and thus expressions of his faithfulness. Christ's body has "need of you" because of the unique ways you help the whole body experience the manifold, gracious love of God.

PRAYER

Father, once again I revel in the wisdom with which you designed the body of Christ and my limited role in it, which in its very limits affords me the most opportunities to give and receive your love. Help me today to give and receive as much of your love as possible. In Jesus' name, amen.

MEDITATE MORE

Review 1 Corinthians 12 to refresh yourself on the brilliant ways God designed Christ's body to maximize every member's experience of God's grace.

| *God is able to make all grace abound to you, so that having all sufficiency in all things at all times, you may abound in every good work.* 2 CORINTHIANS 9:8

All Sufficiency in All Things at All Times

GOD IS FAITHFUL . . . TO MAKE ALL GRACE ABOUND TO YOU

God makes this astounding promise to those who wish to become truly rich.

To be rich is to have a wealth of resources at your disposal to pursue what you believe will make you most satisfied and fulfilled now and into the foreseeable future. To become rich, first you must understand what kind of wealth you're pursuing and how the economy functions that generates this wealth. Second, you must wisely invest in that economy, whether you're pursuing wealth in the world's economies or God's economy.

The world is full of counsel on how to use its economies to accumulate money and benefit from what it can do for you. But God's economy functions very differently from the world's, and if you want to benefit from what God can do for you, you must look to the Bible.

In 2 Corinthians 8–9, Paul describes how God's beautiful economy of generous grace works to produce a wealth of joy, gratitude, faith, and "all sufficiency [for all saints] in all things at all times [for] every good work."

First, he points to the example of the Macedonian Christians, who, though living in "extreme poverty," experienced an "abundance of joy" in their salvation, which "overflowed in a wealth of generosity" in their contribution to the poor in Jerusalem (2 Cor. 8:2). Then Paul points to the example of Jesus, who, "though he was rich, yet for [their] sake he became poor, so that [they] by his poverty might become rich" (2 Cor. 8:9).

Here's how the divine economic cycle works. When we receive God's free, generous grace, it produces joy in us. This joy in freely receiving God's grace moves us to generously give grace to others. Our generosity "is not only supplying the needs of the saints but is also overflowing in many thanksgivings to God" (2 Cor. 9:12). This puts us in the position of trusting him to supply all our needs (Phil. 4:19), which he does in ways that increase our faith and multiply more thanksgivings to God. But as with any economy, the size of our return depends on the size of our investment: "Whoever sows sparingly will also reap sparingly, and whoever sows bountifully will also reap bountifully" (2 Cor. 9:6). Each person is free to "give as he has decided in his heart, not reluctantly or under compulsion, for God loves a cheerful giver" (2 Cor. 9:7).

If we trust in God and invest generously in his economy by giving to meet the needs of others, then "he who supplies seed to the sower and bread for food will [faithfully] supply and multiply your seed for sowing and increase the harvest of your righteousness. You will be enriched in every way to be generous in every way, which through us will produce thanksgiving to God" (2 Cor. 9:10–11).

That's how we become truly rich. In God's economy of grace, generous giving to meet the needs of others is the investment that produces the return of increased joy, gratitude, and faith—for ourselves and others. And if we're willing to make this investment, God promises to faithfully make all his grace abound to us so we will have *all sufficiency* in *all things* at *all times* for *every good work* he gives us to do.

PRAYER

Father, thank you for this truly astounding promise: you are "able to make all grace abound to [me], so that having all sufficiency in all things at all times, [I] may abound in every good work." Because I want to be truly rich—rich in joy (Ps. 16:11), "abounding in thanksgiving" (Col. 2:7), "rich in faith" (James 2:5), and "rich in good works" (1 Tim. 6:18)—give me faith to invest in your economy of grace that I may be "enriched in every way to be generous in every way." In Jesus' name, amen.

MEDITATE MORE

Read 2 Corinthians 9.

44

O God, you are my God; earnestly I seek you; my soul thirsts for you; my flesh faints for you, as in a dry and weary land where there is no water. PSALM 63:1

More, God!

GOD IS FAITHFUL . . . TO GIVE YOU AN UNQUENCHABLE THIRST

Have you ever wondered why Moses pleaded with God, "Please show me your glory" (Ex. 33:18) *after* experiencing unsurpassed theophanies? Moses had encountered God in the burning bush, the signs in Egypt, the Red Sea deliverance, the pillars of cloud and fire, the miraculous wilderness provisions, the miraculous victory over the Amalekites, his visions on Mount Sinai, and God directly speaking to him in great detail all along the way. We might wish to ask Moses, "What more do you want?" I imagine Moses would have answered something like, "More of God's glory, of course. I've barely glimpsed it." And he would have been right.

Then there's David, who also pleaded with God, "Make me to know your ways, O LORD; teach me your paths. Lead me in your truth and teach me" (Ps. 25:4–5)—this *after* God dramatically chose him "from the sheepfolds" to be Israel's king (Ps. 78:70), promised him an eternal kingdom (2 Sam. 7:13), prospered nearly everything he did, delivered him repeatedly from conspiring enemies, and guided him all along the way. We might wish to ask David, "What more do you want?" I imagine he too would have answered something like, "To know more of God's ways, of course. I've grasped so little." And he would have been right.

Great saints are characterized by a deep soul-longing for God (Ps. 63:1), a thirst to be near him like a deer thirsts for water (Ps. 42:1). Such longing made Moses a friend of God (Ex. 33:11) and made David a man after God's own heart (1 Sam. 13:14). For the highest good any saint will ever experience is to be near God (Ps. 73:28).

To encounter the living God is to glimpse the Source of all joy and pleasure (Ps. 16:11), all hope (Rom. 15:13), all power (Rev. 1:8), and indestructible life (Heb. 7:16). It is to glimpse "the place where all the beauty came from."[18] And such a glimpse of infinite glory can only leave us longing for more.

This is a wonderful longing. For "none honors God like the thirst of desire."[19] Why? Because God is the fountain of all satisfaction. And "the best way to glorify a fountain is to get down on your empty hands with your thirsty soul and put your face in the water, and suck life, and then look up and say, 'Ah.'"[20]

To know and love God is to long to know and love him more. For if you really know him in some measure, it implies that he has faithfully made himself known to you (Matt. 16:17). And if you really love him in some measure, it implies that he faithfully loved you first (1 John 4:19). God's great longing is for you to be with him where he is, to show you more of his glory forever (John 17:24). That's why your soul thirsts for him, and why your thirst will never be fully quenched in this age.

PRAYER

Father, "you are my God; earnestly I seek you; my soul thirsts for you." And thank you for so faithfully giving me the priceless gift of this unquenchable thirst for more of you, my inconsolable longing to be with you where you are, "the place where all the beauty came from." Show me more of your glory and let me know more of your ways! In Jesus' name, amen.

MEDITATE MORE

Read Psalm 63.

| *Draw near to God, and he will draw near to you.* JAMES 4:8

Your Invitation to Intimacy with God

GOD IS FAITHFUL . . . TO INVITE YOU TO DRAW NEAR TO HIM

God's nearness. It's the best taste of heaven we can have on earth. That's why for us "it is good to be near God" (Ps. 73:28). And to be near him is to experience intimacy with him.

To be intimate with someone is to really *know* and *be known* by them. We frequently use proximity language to describe it. An intimate friend is someone we feel *close* to. If something happens that damages this intimacy, they feel *distant* from us. But of course, relational intimacy isn't dependent on proximity. We can sit close to someone who feels distant *and* feel close to someone four thousand miles away.

This is as true in our relationship with God as it is with anyone else. God's nearness or distance doesn't describe his actual proximity to us, since "he is actually not far from each one of us" (Acts 17:27). But for billions of people, he might as well be light years away. Even many Christians experience him as distant. So what draws us near to God and he to us?

Some believe that accurate knowledge about God is the key. Knowledge *is* crucial, since "increasing in the knowledge of God" pleases God (Col. 1:10), and Jesus pointed out that many vainly worship what they do not know (John 4:22). But speaking to those in his day who possessed the most scriptural knowledge, Jesus also said, "You search the Scriptures because you think that in them you have eternal life; and it is they that bear witness about me, yet you refuse to come to me that you may have life" (John 5:39–40). And today, we have more good Bible translations and supporting resources available to the average person than ever, especially to Western Christians. But we're not abounding in Enochs, people who intimately walk with God

(Gen. 5:24). Why? Because true knowledge *about* God doesn't necessarily produce a true knowledge *of* God.

What does produce an intimate knowledge of God? Here's what Jesus said: "Whoever has my commandments and keeps them, he it is who loves me. And he who loves me will be loved by my Father, and I will love him and manifest myself to him" (John 14:21). And David wrote, "The friendship of the LORD is for those who fear him, and he makes known to them his covenant" (Ps. 25:14). God is intimate with those who truly *love him*. And those who truly love him truly *trust him*. And those who truly trust him truly *obey him*—which is what fearing him means. For "the fear of the LORD is the beginning of knowledge" (Prov. 1:7).

Intimacy with God—true knowledge *of* God springing from and deepening our love for him—is most often fostered through what encourages us (or seems to force us) to trust him most in order to obey him. Which is why James and Peter tell us to rejoice in trials that test our faith (James 1:2–4; 1 Peter 1:7–9). Because in this age, trials, like little else, call forth in us love-fueled faith and obedience of faith through which God manifests himself and his covenant love to us.

Your trials are God's invitation for you to draw near to him, so you might experience the best taste of heaven you can have on earth: God drawing near to you.

PRAYER

Father, I long for your nearness, my best taste of heaven on earth. So, grant me whatever it takes to encourage me to draw near to you through love-fueled trust and obedience through which you will draw near to me through your Holy Spirit. In Jesus' name, amen.

MEDITATE MORE

Read John 14:15–26. What is the Holy Spirit's role in God manifesting himself to you?

There Is No Intimacy without Trembling

GOD IS FAITHFUL . . . TO TEACH YOU TO FEAR HIM

In the previous chapter, we reflected on why Christians have a God-given, unquenchable thirst to be near God. It is a wonderful longing. But as this verse says, "The friendship of the Lord is [only] for those who fear him."

Fear him? Doesn't Scripture say that "perfect love casts out fear" (1 John 4:18)? Yes, it casts out the fear of God's condemnation—that's the fear the apostle John was addressing. But the fear our text refers to is what John experienced when he encountered the risen Son of God on Patmos which caused him to fall "at his feet as though dead" (Rev. 1:17).

John was by no means alone in this fearful experience of intimacy with the Almighty. Remember when Moses prayed, "Please show me your glory" (Ex. 33:18)? God granted this request, but still only revealed a further glimpse, since, as he told Moses, "Man shall not see me and live" (Ex. 33:20–23). But even just a further glimpse caused this friend of God to fall on his face in reverent fear (Ex. 34:8). This is true for saints throughout Scripture who experienced the most intimacy with God: they glimpsed both his wonderful tenderness and his fearful holiness.

God is the kindest person in existence, and the most severe. In Christ, he is both "gentle and lowly" (Matt. 11:29) and "the Almighty" whose wrath is terrifying (Rev. 1:8; 6:15–17). He is the "friend . . . of sinners" (Luke 7:34), but only of "those who fear him" (Ps. 25:14).

This should not discourage you from seeking greater intimacy with God. No, God wants you to draw near to him (James 4:8). His nearness really is our greatest good (Ps. 73:28). But obtaining our greatest good usually requires more from us than we imagine. God is too good and too faithful to allow evil in us to go unaddressed. His holiness will not allow our unholiness to rest in peace. Our greatest Friend loved us with the greatest possible love by laying down his life for us to cover our sins (John 15:13). And he loves us enough to discipline us in order to wean us off of sinful pleasures and desires, and increase our longing for real, lasting, unsurpassable pleasures that are available to those who fear him enough to draw near to him (1 Peter 1:6–9).

And though "for the moment [his] discipline seems painful rather than pleasant, . . . later it yields the peaceful fruit of righteousness to those who have been trained by it" (Heb. 12:11). It's often more painful than we expect or wish, but the peaceful fruit will be far sweeter than we expect or wish.

So, pray with all your heart, like Moses and David, for more: more glory, more understanding, more intimacy, more nearness. And know that it will require more than you think. But remember, the intimate "friendship of the Lord is for those who fear him" (Ps. 25:14). There is no intimacy with God without trembling before God.

PRAYER

Yes, Father, show me more of your glory, give me more understanding of your ways, make me your intimate friend, drawing nearer to me. And I understand that there is no intimacy with you without trembling before you. So, whatever it takes, teach me to appropriately fear you. In Jesus' name, amen.

MEDITATE MORE

Read Proverbs 9:10. Why is the fear of the Lord the beginning of wisdom?

Why, O Lord, Do You Stand Far Away?

God Is Faithful . . . to Show You How to Faithfully Lament

*T*hat's a remarkable thing to say to God. Since this prayer is in Scripture, we can assume it isn't sinful. But should a saint who loves and trusts and treasures God above all else ever pray this way? How is this not an expression of unbelief?

That's an important question. This psalm, as do at least one-third of all biblical psalms, teaches us how to faithfully *lament*.

This psalmist is lamenting his agonizing bewilderment over unjust, greedy, violent acts against innocent, helpless people. He's not only disturbed by the wicked acts he's witnessed; he's disturbed that the wicked are prospering from their wickedness (Ps. 10:1–11). We can sense his righteous anger. Such horrible oppression and injustice should make him (and us) angry.

But he's also troubled that his biblically informed understanding of God's character does not seem to match the reality he's observing. He believes "God is a righteous judge" (Ps. 7:11) who "executes justice" for the helpless and vulnerable (Deut. 10:18). But he's *not seeing* justice executed for the helpless and vulnerable. He's *seeing* the wicked oppressor "prosper at all times" (Ps. 10:5). Why God is allowing this injustice to continue is beyond him.

So, the psalmist faithfully turns to God with his burning indignation toward evil perpetrators and his tearful compassion toward victims. And *because* he desires God to fulfill his promises to bring about justice and deliverance, he's doing with God what we all do with those we love deeply who behave in ways we don't understand: honestly express his confusion and pain.

When the psalmist asks God why he seems distant or hidden, he's not blaming God or scolding God for neglecting his responsibilities. He's describing how this terrible situation appears to him from his finite perspective, especially because he cares so deeply for the glory of God's name as well as the faith of God's people.

We too witness, and sometimes are victims of, such wicked injustices. Righteous anger is a faithful response to real evil. A lack of such anger, if it's a manifestation of indifference, is an unfaithful response. And if we observe an apparent discontinuity between what we know of God from the Scriptures and what we observe in the world, and we're not painfully perplexed, it might indicate an unfaithful indifference to God's glory. A righteous anger toward perpetrators, a righteous compassion for afflicted victims, and a righteous desire for God to fulfill his righteous promises faithfully overflow in a prayer of lament to the God in whom we hope (Ps. 43:5) and from whom we receive hope (Ps. 62:5).

When the mystery of God's providential purposes meets the finiteness of our understanding and it doesn't make sense to us, God faithfully shows us how to respond through Psalm 10. God wants us to cry out in prayer to him precisely because we love and trust and treasure him above all else. And because another aspect of the mystery of God's providential purposes is that he ordains such prayers as the means through which he responds and brings such evils to an end.

PRAYER

Father, thank you for faithfully including Psalm 10 in Scripture to help teach me how to pray at terrible moments when evil people seem to prosper, and you seem to be distant. In such moments, give me sufficient grace to trust your promises over my perceptions, and at the same time, grace to turn my righteous anger, compassion, and love for your glory into the right kind of prayer of lament. In Jesus' name, amen.

MEDITATE MORE

Read Psalm 10. How does the psalmist both honestly express his anger and confusion and express his faith that God will keep his promises?

I Believe; Help My Unbelief!

GOD IS FAITHFUL . . . TO HELP YOUR UNBELIEF

This was the prayer of a desperate father who had come to Jesus to intercede on behalf of his afflicted child. It expresses in five simple words a profound, difficult, confusing, and common experience. All followers of Jesus have both belief and unbelief, both faith and doubt, present in us at the same time.

The father of the afflicted boy in Mark 9 no doubt had an experience-informed vulnerability to his unbelief. He had spent years caring for his son, saving him from death numerous times. Which means he, and we can assume his wife, lived with the daily dread that next time they might not be there in time.

Imagine the fatigue of the continual vigilance night and day. Imagine the recurring relational strain on their marriage that often accompanies stressful and painful parenting situations. Imagine the ways their son's affliction affected them financially, from the expense of seeking help for him to the lost income from having less time devoted to earning a living. And overshadowing all that, imagine the cultural shame they endured, wondering how they or their child had sinned and brought this curse upon him, and knowing others likely wondered the same thing (as in John 9:1–2).

Surely this beleaguered father had prayed often for his priceless son, with no visible results, and had sought out other spiritual experts to drive the devil out, but to no avail.

Stories of Jesus' power over disease and demons stirred in him enough hope to bring his child to Jesus. Not finding the famous rabbi, he had asked Jesus' disciples for help, but they were no more effective than anyone else had been. We can understand why his faith was ebbing low when Jesus showed up and he pleaded, "If you can do anything, have compassion on us and help us" (v. 22).

Jesus' response was startling: "'If you can'! All things are possible for one who believes" (v. 23). It seemed to surprise this father. It surprises us. We might have expected Jesus to comfort this man, but instead he rebukes him. It makes us wonder, is this how Jesus feels about our unbelief?

That this father had sought Jesus out shows there was faith in his request. But there was also unbelief; part of him doubted Jesus would be successful where everyone else had failed. But Jesus isn't like the others. Jesus is God the Son. "And without faith it is impossible to please him, for whoever would draw near to God must believe that he exists and that he rewards those who seek him" (Heb. 11:6). Experience-informed unbelief is still unbelief.

Jesus, being the good physician, does not coddle unbelief, just like a good doctor doesn't coddle cancer in a patient. If left invisible and untreated, it will kill. So, what Jesus does is help this struggling father clearly see his sin of unbelief.

And it worked. We see this in the father's desperate cry to Jesus: "I believe; help my unbelief!" Jesus faithfully honored the father's faith, however feeble, and set the boy free (Mark 9:25–27).

In the next chapter, we'll explore further the dangers of unbelief and why Jesus' response to this father was a faithful one. But for now, let's just let this story work on us and confront any experience-informed unbelief lurking inside us.

PRAYER

Father, thank you for preserving in Scripture this startling account of Jesus' faithful response to this struggling father. You see where experience-informed unbelief lurks in me, even if I don't. Do what you must to confront it. Help my unbelief! In Jesus' name, amen.

MEDITATE MORE

Read this entire story in Mark 9:14–29. At one point Jesus said, "O faithless generation, how long am I to be with you? How long am I to bear with you?" (v. 19). Why did he say this?

How Jesus Helps Your Unbelief

GOD IS FAITHFUL . . . TO HELP UNBLOCK YOUR CHANNELS TO GOD'S GRACE

In the last chapter, we observed Jesus surprisingly confront unbelief in a father who had asked him to heal his son. As we examine why Jesus did this, let's keep in mind that unbelief is a common temptation. But it is spiritually dangerous since it can lead us "to fall away from the living God" (Heb. 3:12). It is an enemy we must fight vigorously. It is a cancer that must be treated aggressively.

We each fight unique battles against unbelief because each of us has unique experiences and unique temperaments that make us uniquely vulnerable to certain forms of unbelief. Receiving help to see our vulnerabilities to unbelief is crucial to winning our battles. And it is something Jesus is happy to help us with if we ask him.

The father in Mark 9 was very much like us. His unbelief had roots in his unique experience. So does ours. His fears and disappointments shaped his expectations. So do ours. He was vulnerable, in deeply personal places, to losing the fight for faith. So are we. We can sympathize with this man when he pleaded with Jesus, "If you can do anything, have compassion on us and help us" (v. 22), because we've probably prayed or thought similar things.

And here's what we need to remember: Jesus' rebuke to a believer who is allowing unbelief to infect and enfeeble his faith and govern his behavior is a great mercy. Faith is the channel through which God's graces of salvation and sanctification and spiritual gifts all flow. Unbelief obstructs the channel and therefore inhibits the flow of God's grace (James 1:5–8). So, Jesus' rebuke of the man's unbelief is the mercifully painful, momentary discipline of the Lord intended to expose the sin of unbelief so the believer can see it for what it is and fight it; because if he doesn't, he will not share the Lord's holiness and will not bear the "peaceful fruit of righteousness" (Heb. 12:10–11).

All of us who believe in Jesus also have unbelief in Jesus. It's not surprising, because we all live with deceitful, indwelling sin (Heb. 3:13). And we all live in a fallen, deceitful world. So, we all must frequently fight for faith (1 Tim. 6:12) by battling unbelief.

But the presence of unbelief in us is often subtle. We don't always see it clearly. It has roots in our unique experiences and in our unique temperaments, which make us uniquely vulnerable to its deceitfulness. Our doubts can seem reasonable to us, even justifiable. But like all sin and fallenness, unbelief is spiritually dangerous. What we really need, even though we might prefer to avoid it, is for Jesus to mercifully help us see our unbelief, even if it means his momentarily painful discipline.

And he will faithfully answer you. He answers the prayer, "I believe; help my unbelief!" And the way he'll help you fight it is by exposing it, that doubt you want to conceal or can't see. But do not fear his discipline; fear unbelief. Unbelief blocks the channels of grace that flow through faith. It will rob you of joy and, if left unaddressed, it will destroy you. The momentary pain of God's loving discipline, however, is the path to greater joy, for it opens the channels to more of God's grace—to more of God.

PRAYER

Father, thank you for loving me too much to allow unbelief to remain unaddressed in me. I don't want it to block any channel through which I can receive any available grace from you. So again I invite your loving, faithful discipline if that is the best way for you to help my unbelief. In Jesus' name, amen.

MEDITATE MORE

Read John 20:24–29. How did Jesus respond to his disciple Thomas's declaration, "I will never believe"? Why?

50

For we do not want you to be unaware, brothers, of the affliction we experienced in Asia. For we were so utterly burdened beyond our strength that we despaired of life itself. Indeed, we felt that we had received the sentence of death. But that was to make us rely not on ourselves but on God who raises the dead. 2 CORINTHIANS 1:8–9

When You're Burdened beyond Your Strength

GOD IS FAITHFUL ... TO COMFORT YOU WITH A HOPE STRONGER THAN DEATH

Paul wrote the letter we know as 2 Corinthians right on the tail end of an experience of severe suffering. He doesn't specify what his affliction was, though it likely was significant persecution nearly to the point of execution. But in the merciful, faithful wisdom of the Holy Spirit, the specifics are withheld to encourage us all to apply Paul's words to "any affliction" (2 Cor. 1:4).

But which of our sufferings qualify as sharing in Christ's sufferings? Paul provides an answer when he says the "God of all comfort . . . comforts us in *all our affliction,* so that we may be able to comfort those who are in *any affliction*" (2 Cor. 1:3–4). *All* and *any* are comprehensive words.

A sampling of biblical affliction includes illness and death (like Lazarus in John 11 and Epaphroditus in Philippians 2), the experience of spiritual desertion in Psalm 22, the disillusioning confusion of Psalm 89 when it appears God isn't keeping his promises, the disorientation of significant doubt expressed in Psalm 73, or in Psalm 88, the agony of prolonged and dark depression.

All these experiences and more are forms of suffering. What makes "all our affliction" a sharing in Christ's sufferings is that when they befall us, we turn in faith to him on whom "we have set our hope" for the deliverance he intends to provide for us (2 Cor. 1:10).

And this brings us to the valuable lesson we learn from Paul. His suffering brought him to the end of himself: not just to the end of his bodily strength, but to the end of his earthly hopes and plans. He thought this affliction would kill him. When Paul stared death in the face, what gave him hope? The "God who raises the dead."

Although we know Paul was delivered from this particular "deadly peril" (2 Cor. 1:10), his deliverance from death wasn't the primary comfort he received from God. Nor was it that he'd be able to comfort others "in any affliction." His primary comfort was that at the very end, when death finally arrives, there is one, great, death-defying hope for the Christian: God will raise him from the dead.

Sometimes, it requires afflictions to reveal what we're truly hoping in. God doesn't enjoy afflicting his children (Lam. 3:33), but, when necessary, our loving, faithful Father will allow us to be burdened beyond our strength, perhaps to the point of despairing of life itself, so we can receive from the "God of all comfort" a hope and joy far beyond what the world can offer (Heb. 12:7–11).

Whatever it takes to help us experience this comfort, to help us set our real, ultimate hope on God, is worth it. It really is. I speak from some experience when I say the comfort God brings through such a season infuses all temporal comforts with a hope that transcends them. And when all earthly comforts finally fail, this hope will be the one comfort that remains.

PRAYER

Father, thank you for being the "God of all comfort," especially of the unsurpassable comfort and hope that comes from your promise of giving me eternal life. Grant to me, according to your wise, loving, faithful judgment, whatever will help root my deepest hope and most profound comfort in you as the God who raises the dead. In Jesus' name, amen.

MEDITATE MORE

Read 2 Corinthians 1:1–11. What changes would result in the way you live if you experienced the hope Paul describes?

51

"What you are doing is not good. . . . Now obey my voice; I will give you advice, and God be with you!". . . So Moses listened to the voice of his father-in-law and did all that he had said.

EXODUS 18:17, 19, 24

When God Sends You a Jethro

GOD IS FAITHFUL . . . EVEN IN WHAT HE DOESN'T SAY

God is as faithful in what he chooses *not to say* as he is in what he chooses to say. Let me give you an example.

In Exodus 18, Jethro, Moses' father-in-law, paid his now-famous son-in-law a visit. After hearing Moses' amazing report, "Jethro rejoiced for all the good that the LORD had done to Israel, in that he had delivered them out of the hand of the Egyptians" (v. 9).

The next day, Jethro got to watch his son-in-law in action, and this left him amazed in a different way. "Moses sat to judge the people, and the people stood around Moses from morning till evening" (v. 13). After asking some questions, Jethro said, "What you are doing is not good. You and the people with you will certainly wear yourselves out, for the thing is too heavy for you. You are not able to do it alone" (vv. 17–18). He then proceeded to give Moses some sage advice on how to delegate his judicial responsibilities, and "Moses listened to the voice of his father-in-law and did all that he had said" (v. 24).

Now, why didn't God just tell Moses that from the beginning? After all, God would "speak to Moses face to face, as a man speaks to his friend" (Ex. 33:11). He gave Moses many detailed verbal instructions about things like the construction of the tabernacle and the keeping of the law. Why didn't he instruct Moses on how to structure a judicial system? Why let Moses struggle under an overbearing workload until he finally sent Jethro to advise him?

I think one important reason is that God understands how influential his word is. And he does not intend the vast majority of our methods or systems to be considered sacred and therefore unalterable. So even if he approves of them, he doesn't want to give them the weight of scriptural revelation.

There are countless ways to do things depending on our context and technology. But if this counsel had come directly from God's mouth rather

than from Jethro, we likely would still be structuring our churches, denom-
inations, and organizations by thousands, hundreds, fifties, and tens (Ex.
18:21) because we would assume this was "God's way" of organizing people.

God is faithful to speak with clarity and precision regarding everything
that's required to redeem his people and make them holy throughout the
generations. He's clear on every commandment to be obeyed and every
promise to be trusted. But regarding secondary or administrative things,
he leaves much to our figuring out. He is faithful to answer our prayers for
guidance in these areas, but he almost always answers indirectly, because he
doesn't want us to make an idol out of what is only meant to be helpful.

God is very wise. He's as faithful in what he chooses not to say as he is
in what he chooses to say. So, in our prayers for strategic and administrative
wisdom, we should expect God to faithfully send us Jethros and not some
special revelation.

PRAYER

*Father, thank you for being as faithful in what you don't explicitly explain
to me as what you do. Wherever I need guidance in an area you choose not
to address, send me the Jethro I need. In Jesus' name, amen.*

MEDITATE MORE

Read Exodus 18 and note not only Jethro's wise counsel, but Moses' remarkable humility in receiving it.

52

"I know your works. You have the reputation of being alive, but you are dead. Wake up, and strengthen what remains and is about to die, for I have not found your works complete in the sight of my God." REVELATION 3:1–2

Escape the Prideful Prison of an Undeserved Reputation

GOD IS FAITHFUL . . . TO CONFRONT YOUR HYPOCRISY

It is true that "a good name is to be chosen rather than great riches" (Prov. 22:1). But that's only true to the extent that our good name, our reputation, accurately represents who we are. If we cultivate and promote a reputation for ourselves that is better than we actually are, God has a scathing term for us: hypocrite.

Hypocrisy includes maintaining and promoting a reputation that we once deserved but now do not. In the text above, Jesus was addressing the Christians in the city of Sardis who had a reputation for being alive because once they had been. But now they were a shadow of their former selves, and their reputation was a lingering echo of past vitality. So, Jesus' rebuke is a literal "wake-up" call.

Why did they need Jesus' rebuke? Hadn't they noticed their spiritual decline? Didn't they discern their hypocrisy? Well, if those Christians were anything like you and me, they probably did to some degree. But spiritual decline usually occurs in a series of subtle compromises which we rationalize, so we often don't fully perceive our true condition.

At that point, our reputations add to the deceptive distortion. We can easily believe that if others see us as "alive," perhaps it's true. But even if we are cognizant of the dissonance, we find it very hard to admit this to those who hold us in higher esteem than we deserve. But in hiding behind our reputation to escape social shame, we convert it into a prison of pride. And the longer we pretend to be who we used to be, the harder it becomes to admit and the more our integrity deteriorates. Eventually we become "dead," even without fully realizing it, because we still have "the reputation of being alive." We often don't see our true condition until someone truly mirrors it back to us.

This is what Jesus, the "faithful witness" (Rev. 1:5), did for the Sardisian Christians. His true words hurt, but were full of grace, for "faithful are the wounds of a friend" (Prov. 27:6). He told them, "I know your works," reminding them (and us) that "all are naked and exposed to [his] eyes" (Heb. 4:13). Then he exhorted them to (1) "wake up," (2) "strengthen what remains and is about to die," (3) "remember . . . what [they] received and heard," and (4) "keep it, and repent" (Rev. 3:2–3). Then Jesus gave them a warning and promise: whoever would "not wake up" would face his severe judgment (Rev. 3:3), but whoever heeded his warning, he would "never blot his name out of the book of life" (Rev. 3:5).

Let us also hear what the faithful Spirit of our "faithful witness" said to the Sardisian Christians, if perchance he's saying it to us. For we aren't who we want to think we are or who other people think we are. All we truly are is who we are before God. And repentance and returning to faithfulness is the only escape from the destruction of continuing down the deceptive road of spiritual compromise while hypocritically concealing it behind an undeserved reputation. "Today, if you hear his voice, do not harden your hearts" (Heb. 4:7).

PRAYER

Father, thank you for the mercifully hard words of your faithful Son. I confess that I'm prone to the same hypocrisy the Sardisian Christians succumbed to and feel the temptation to conceal sin and spiritual decline behind an inflated reputation. If this has any hold on me, wake me up, whatever it takes, and give me grace to humbly repent and return to the faithful road. In Jesus' name, amen.

MEDITATE MORE

Read Revelation 3:1–6 to hear Jesus' full rebuke, full warning, and full promise.

God Knows

GOD IS FAITHFUL . . . TO KNOW YOUR SUFFERING
AND TIME OF YOUR DELIVERANCE

At the beginning of the book of Exodus, the people of Israel are in Egypt, caught in the oppressive, abusive death grip of slavery and crying out for deliverance. But chapter 2 ends with two words that are pregnant with hope: *God knew.*

God knew each person's suffering: each dehumanizing degradation, each bodily injury, each person's trauma, and each person's anger fueled by his hopeless situation that for at least one person boiled over into violence against oppressors (Ex. 2:11–12), and for others into violence against members of his oppressed community (Ex. 2:13).

God knew. And he was preparing to act in a way that would leave a permanent, indelible imprint upon the collective memory of the human race.

But God didn't only know what was happening, God *foreknew* that it was going to happen. Centuries earlier, God had told Abraham, Israel's founding father, that his offspring would be "sojourners in a land that is not theirs," where they would "be afflicted for four hundred years," after which he'd judge their oppressors, and Israel would "come out with great possessions" (Gen. 15:13–14).

But God's revealed foreknowledge also revealed a divine purpose in Israel's agonizing experience that extended beyond Israel. For two verses later, God told Abraham his descendants would then return to Canaan "in the fourth generation, for the iniquity of the Amorites is not yet complete" (Gen. 15:16). This statement about the Amorites is a multilayered gift for the saints of God because it reveals that *God knew what he was doing.*

God's purposes and timing were not just about Israel and Egypt; they were also about God's righteous judgment on the Canaanite peoples. When the time was ripe for him to fulfill his covenant to Abraham, it would also be ripe to bring judgment on "the iniquity of the Amorites." The reason this revelation is a gift to God's saints is that it tells us there are factors relating to our afflictions and agonizing situations extending beyond us. Like the enslaved Israelites, God's delay might seem like God's neglect, but it isn't. He just knows what he's doing.

Therefore, the words "God knew" are filled with hope. Your affliction has a purpose and a timeline, though you likely don't know what either is yet. But someday you will understand that the purposes for both your affliction and how long you were required to endure it extended far beyond the range of your perception. And then it will make sense.

Jesus Christ has guaranteed your exodus, not only from your afflictions, but from your sojourn in this foreign land (Heb. 11:13). And when you reach the true promised land, no matter what you suffered in this vale of tears, you will have no regrets. God will have worked everything for such glorious good (Rom. 8:28) that all your affliction will seem light and momentary in comparison (2 Cor. 4:17).

In your suffering, cry out to God for help (Ex. 2:23). He faithfully hears. And when the time is right, you will see his faithful deliverance. For God sees you—and *he knows*.

PRAYER

Father, thank you for what Exodus 2:25 and Genesis 15:13–16 reveal regarding what you know about me right now, and how what you foreknow about everything informs the timing of your answers to my prayers. Help me remember this when I most need it. In Jesus' name, amen.

MEDITATE MORE

Read Acts 2:22–32 and ponder all that was involved in the most consequential "definite plan and foreknowledge of God" (v. 23).

The Insanity of Trusting Yourself

GOD IS FAITHFUL . . . TO HUMBLE THE PRIDE OF HUMAN WISDOM

God is at war with human wisdom: "I will destroy the wisdom of the wise, and the discernment of the discerning I will thwart" (1 Cor. 1:19). The Spirit speaking through the apostle Paul goes even further: "Since, in the wisdom of God, the world did not know God through wisdom, it pleased God through the folly of what we preach to save those who believe" (1 Cor. 1:21). What does God have against human wisdom?

In this chapter, we'll go way back to the cataclysm in Eden to see what mere human wisdom has done to God and to us. In the next chapter, we'll examine why God engineered our redemption to humble human wisdom and restore it to its proper place.

The first man and woman ate fruit from the tree of the knowledge of good and evil, the only food God forbade them to eat. It was his only prohibition, in fact. They knew him as a Father who overwhelmingly said yes to them. So why did they eat the one forbidden thing? Because the serpent told them God was misleading them about his one no.

Never mind that God had created the glorious world they inhabited, provided them life, breath, and everything, and trusting him had resulted in their profound happiness. Never mind that in his one prohibition, God had conferred upon them the profound dignity of moral agency, the choice to love him, trust him, and accept his authority or not.

The serpent had come to encourage them to choose the "or not" option. He told them God had hidden a treasure in the fruit that would grant them near divine status: "God knows that when you eat of it your eyes will be opened, and you will be like God, knowing good and evil" (Gen. 3:5). If they ate the fruit, they would be free from perpetual intellectual dependency on God—they could think on their own, for themselves.

In their desire for wisdom, they didn't consider that to handle such knowledge, one must possess the capacities to comprehend all possible options and contingencies (omniscience), to always choose the right course of action based on omniscience combined with perfect righteousness (omni-wisdom), and to make reality conform to the right course of righteous action determined by an omni-judicial omniscience (omnipotence).

So, they chose not to love, trust, and obey their omniscient, omni-wise, omnipotent Creator, but to lean on their own understanding. They ate the fruit.

God was true to his word: "the eyes of both were opened" (Gen. 3:7). But the serpent wasn't true to his word: the knowledge did not make them God-like; it only made them miserable, being infinitely beyond what they were designed to bear. And all of us have been laboring under its crushing weight ever since.

This is what God has against mere human wisdom, our rebellious and insane inclination to distrust him, our "faithful Creator" (1 Peter 4:19), and lean on our own minuscule understanding, which only leads to our destruction. As we'll see in the next chapter, our merciful, faithful Creator hasn't left us to our foolish selves, but has devised a way to redeem us that allows us to hand him back the fruit.

PRAYER

Father, forgive me for every time I've indulged my insane, sinful inclination to distrust you and lean on my own understanding. And thank you for your infinite mercy and faithfulness in rescuing me from my sinful self. In Jesus' name, amen.

MEDITATE MORE

Read 1 Corinthians 1:18–31. How is "the foolishness of God . . . wiser than men, and the weakness of God . . . stronger than men" (1 Cor. 1:25)?

> *Has not God made foolish the wisdom of the world? For since, in the wisdom of God, the world did not know God through wisdom, it pleased God through the folly of what we preach to save those who believe.* 1 CORINTHIANS 1:20-21

The Sanity of Handing Back the Fruit

GOD IS FAITHFUL . . . TO SAVE US THROUGH THE FOLLY OF THE GOSPEL

When God created us, he designed us to think *for ourselves*, meaning he didn't want automatons, but intelligent beings with the capacity for moral agency. That's one reason the tree of the knowledge of good and evil was present in the garden. But God did not design us to think *by ourselves*, meaning without him. For very limited, contingent creatures like us need the guidance of our omniscient, omni-wise, omnipotent Creator to know how to live.

Therefore, it is eminently rational for us to trust in the Lord with all our heart. That's wisdom; that's sanity. What's irrational is for us to lean on our own understanding. That's foolishness; that's madness.

That madness, as we saw in the last chapter, was the cataclysm of Eden. We humans traded the wise sanity of thinking *for ourselves* in the safe context of "entrust[ing our] souls to a faithful Creator" (1 Peter 4:19) for the foolish madness of thinking *by ourselves*. Wishing to be wise, we unhinged our reason from our faithful Creator, and became fools (Rom. 1:21).

This is why God is at war with rebellious human wisdom, and why he doesn't permit us to know him through it. To be reconciled to him and redeemed from our fallen state, we must come to him on his terms, not ours. He requires us to hand him back the fruit from the tree of the knowledge of good and evil, that we might once again have access to the tree of life.

He requires this because mere human wisdom is greatly offended that God judges our desire to independently understand and define good and evil as foolish pride requiring humbling. It's greatly offended that God refuses to answer for the evil that ravages this planet—evil that exceeds our comprehension. And it looks at the foolish spectacle of Jesus on the cross, an empty tomb, and the promise of eternal life, and marvels at the idiotic credulity of any who believe these strange things could ever address the most important issues facing the human race. The gospel "is folly to those who are perishing" (1 Cor. 1:18).

But to us who are being saved, this gospel is "the power of God and the wisdom of God" (1 Cor. 1:24). We do not claim to have all our perplexing and agonizing questions answered. But we have come to see that "with God are wisdom and might . . . counsel and understanding" (Job 12:13); that "the fear of the LORD is the beginning of knowledge," but "fools despise wisdom and instruction" (Prov. 1:7); that "whoever trusts in his own mind is a fool, but he who walks in wisdom will be delivered" (Prov. 28:26); that only in God's "light do we see light" (Ps. 36:9). For us, Jesus has become "wisdom from God, righteousness and sanctification and redemption" (1 Cor. 1:30).

This is God's design. He has engineered our redemption to humble human wisdom and restore it to its proper place, where once again we think *for ourselves* under the guidance of our omniscient, omni-wise, omnipotent, faithful Creator. This is true, joyful intellectual freedom, which God mercifully, faithfully, and freely restores to those who are willing to hand back the fruit.

PRAYER

Father, I marvel at your wisdom in not allowing fallen humanity to know you through its rebellious wisdom, and how you engineered the gospel not only to restore to me your righteousness and holiness, but also your wisdom. I happily hand you back the fruit. In Jesus' name, amen.

MEDITATE MORE

Read 1 Corinthians 2 to further marvel over "a wisdom [not] of this age or of the rulers of this age" (1 Cor. 2:6).

56

Therefore I tell you, whatever you ask in prayer, believe that you have received it, and it will be yours. MARK 11:24

Further Up and Further In

GOD IS FAITHFUL . . . TO MAKE PRAYER A STRUGGLE

Of the three primary means of God's grace in the Christian life—his word, prayer, and fellowship—prayer is often the most neglected. Why do we struggle so much to pray?

That question has many answers: we're distractible, we're lazy, we're busy, we've had poor models, we lack a plan, we're overwhelmed by the needs around us, our adversary opposes us, and so on. Any of these might be true of us.

But another significant reason is that many of us find prayer mysterious. We don't understand how it works or, more accurately, we don't understand how it doesn't work. For example, we read promises in Scripture like the one above. Then we pray but we don't see answers. We're left asking, *What's the problem?* And we conclude that either our faith is so pitifully small that God essentially ignores it, or that there must be so many inscrutable, complicating factors obscuring his answers, we end up as prayer agnostics. Either way, we're discouraged from praying much. Mark 11:24 must be for Christians with heroic faith.

But this is not how God wants us to respond to unanswered prayer. He wants us to seriously press into the question, "What's the problem?" Because Jesus' audacious promise above—"whatever you ask in prayer"—is an invitation to an intimate relationship with him.

I know this is a difficult promise for us. I know it exposes our little faith. I know it raises thorny, even grievous questions regarding prayers that have seemed to go unanswered. I know, I know. We're tempted to respond sardonically, "Yeah, 'whatever.'"

Jesus knows it's hard for us too. He knows this promise presses us beyond our limits. He means it to. That's why he made it. He is drawing us beyond what we've yet seen and experienced, and he's calling out a faith in us that we don't think we have and are scared to really exercise. Jesus' purpose isn't to shame us for our little faith; he's inviting us, to borrow a phrase from C. S. Lewis, to "come further up and further in."[21]

When Jesus made this promise, his disciples were marveling that the fig tree Jesus cursed had shriveled up. Writing later, one of them helps us understand what "whatever" means:

> And this is the confidence that we have toward him, that if we ask anything according to his will he hears us. And if we know that he hears us in whatever we ask, we know that we have the requests that we have asked of him. (1 John 5:14–15)

"Whatever" is "anything according to [God's] will." But this is no divine bait-and-switch. This is not a radical promise no one actually experiences. The fig tree really withered. And millions of Christians have received dramatic answers to such prayers.

If "whatever you ask in prayer" hasn't happened yet, don't assume it can't or won't. Don't give up. This promise is an invitation to come further up and further in to knowing God. And many who have taken God up on this invitation testify that God is faithful to his audacious promises if we are audacious enough to believe them.

PRAYER

Father, this audacious promise that whatever I ask you in prayer, if I believe I have received it, will be mine does press me beyond my natural limits. But since it did the same to Jesus' disciples, I don't want to shrink back from it. I want to embrace it and experience the reality of it. I want to "come further up and further in" to the joy of knowing you more. Give me the grace I need to do this today. In Jesus' name, amen.

MEDITATE MORE

Read Mark 11:20–24 and ask God to direct you how he wants you to apply this promise.

"If you abide in me, and my words abide in you, ask whatever you wish, and it will be done for you." JOHN 15:7

Prayer Is Hard Because Relationships Are Hard

GOD IS FAITHFUL . . . TO MAKE PRAYER RELATIONAL, NOT TRANSACTIONAL

This sounds so simple, doesn't it? "Abide in me, and . . . ask whatever you wish." But it is not at all simple, because it is profoundly relational.

Prayer is not a mere service transaction; it is a relational interaction. Faith is not divine currency that we pay God in order to receive "whatever [we] ask in prayer" (Mark 11:24). Faith is a relational response of trust in God and therefore what he promises us. Faith is our saying to God, "I trust you so much that I will live by what you say." Those who really get to know God and learn what it means to *really* trust him are those who really experience the reality Jesus described in this verse. But really getting to know God is no simple thing. And we shouldn't expect it to be.

After all, which of our other deep, intimate relationships are simple? We soon learn how our indwelling sin, our insecurities, and our temperaments complicate our ability to effectively understand and communicate with those we most deeply love. Consider how many resources are devoted to helping us develop effective relational communication. And these are relationships we encounter face-to-face. Should we expect deeply knowing and effectively communicating with God will be less difficult?

Prayer has all the idiosyncrasies of a relationship because it is the most intimate way we interact with God. Like significant human relationships we have, effective communication with God is something we must work hard to learn. It can be perplexing, confusing, frustrating, and mysterious. Relating to God requires more loving intentionality, pursuit, careful listening, humility, persistence, and perseverance than we originally expected or perhaps wanted to give. But, like significant human relationships we have, if we really put in the work, we tend to discover far more about God as a person than we knew before and experience new levels of intimacy and friendship with him. If we don't, we won't.

What examples can we look to? We can look to the Old Testament saints listed in Hebrews 11, who discovered that pressing in to know God was no simple thing, but also discovered that God faithfully "rewards those who seek him" (Heb. 11:6). We can look to the faithful men and women of the New Testament, who discovered pressing in to abide in Jesus was no simple thing, but also discovered that to "know him" was worth having "suffered the loss of all things" (Phil. 3:8–10). And we can look to the great cloud of saints throughout church history who have most seriously taken God at his word—the Adoniram and Ann Judsons, George and Mary Muellers, Hudson and Maria Taylors—who endured the perplexing, confusing, frustrating, mysterious experiences of learning to abide in Christ and have Christ's words abide in them and discovered that they really could ask whatever they wished, and it was done for them.

God is faithful to grant "whatever we wish" on the condition that we "abide in" Jesus. It sounds simple, but it's not. Of course, it's not. Because our most intimate, meaningful relationships are not simple to cultivate and maintain. But they are the most rewarding if we do. That's why prayer has all the idiosyncrasies of a relationship. Because it isn't a service transaction, but a deep, intimate relational interaction.

PRAYER

Father, forgive me for all the times I've thought wrongly about prayer, approaching it more as a transaction than a relational interaction. Whatever it takes, teach me to really abide in Jesus and be so shaped by him that "whatever I wish" aligns with whatever you wish, making your answering my prayer a joy we share together as deep, intimate friends. In Jesus' name, amen.

MEDITATE MORE

Read John 15:1–17, reflecting on each of Jesus' statements on abiding in him.

In His Light Do You See Light?

God Is Faithful . . . to Give You the Light You Need to See

The more I ponder that beautiful sentence from the psalm, the more volumes it speaks. David was a top-tier poet. Let's just ruminate for a moment on what he said about "light."

What is light? We think we know until we're forced to define it. Technically, natural earthy light is the electromagnetic radiance of the sun. But that hardly touches it. There's far more to light than meets the eye.

The same is true of divine light. One way the Bible describes it is the radiance of God's glory (see Rev. 21:23). But again, there's far more to God's light than meets the spiritual "eye."

In the natural realm, sunlight illumines our physical environment, helping us see where to go and revealing myriad dangers around us. It also literally gives and sustains bodily life. Physically speaking, our bodies are products of sunlight, and so is everything that nourishes our bodies. And of course, we'd perish quickly without the heat produced by the sun's radiance.

In the spiritual realm, the same is true of divine light—the light God is (1 John 1:5) and the light God gives (Rev. 21:23–25). God's light illumines our spiritual environment: "The people dwelling in darkness have seen a great light" (Matt. 4:16). It reveals the way to go: "Your word is a lamp to my feet and a light to my path" (Ps. 119:105). And it literally gives and sustains our spiritual life: "God, who said, 'Let light shine out of darkness,' has shone in our hearts to give the light of the knowledge of the glory of God in the face of Jesus Christ" (2 Cor. 4:6).

Natural darkness conceals our physical environment, leaving us easily disoriented and vulnerable to dangers. The same is true of spiritual darkness: we lose our way and can't see our spiritual dangers. But what's different about spiritual darkness is that it masquerades as light (2 Cor. 11:14). "The god of this world" blinds people from seeing God's light (2 Cor. 4:4). So, they think they see their spiritual environment and know where they're going, but they don't. Which is why Jesus said, "If then the light in you is darkness, how great is the darkness!" (Matt. 6:22–23).

But there is incredibly good news for people dwelling in spiritual darkness! Jesus, the light of life (John 8:12) and the life of light (John 1:4), came as "the light of the world" so that we would "not walk in darkness, but . . . have the light of life" (John 8:12). As "the Light," he shows us "the way" to go, reveals "the truth" of our spiritual environment, and gives us "the life" we most long for (John 14:6).

In Jesus, we see the light David wrote of in Psalm 36:9. And in his light, we not only see light, we also become "light in the Lord" (Eph. 5:8) and therefore become ourselves "the light of the world" (Matt. 5:14).

When David wrote that phrase, he knew God as the life-giving light of the world, though he didn't yet know the full revelation of Jesus. But God knew, and faithfully placed this prophetic pointer in David's profound poetry to help us see light in the light of the Light.

PRAYER

Father, thank you for so faithfully sending your Son, the radiance of your glory, as the light of the world, so that I might not walk in darkness but have the light of life and in his light, see light. In Jesus' name, amen.

MEDITATE MORE

Read 2 Corinthians 4:1–6. What does Paul mean by "the light of the knowledge of the glory of God in the face of Jesus Christ" (v. 6)?

59

The LORD is my strength and my song, and he has become my salvation; this is my God, and I will praise him, my father's God, and I will exalt him. EXODUS 15:2

If God Isn't Your Strength, He Won't Be Your Song

GOD IS FAITHFUL . . . WHEN HE PUTS YOU IN WEAK PLACES

God doesn't so much want us to be strong as he wants to be our strength. Which is to say, God wants us to be "strong . . . in the strength of his might" (Eph. 6:10). Because if God isn't our strength, he won't be our song.

Having been miraculously released from slavery and led out of Egypt by Moses, Israel set up camp on the shores of the Red Sea. God had purposefully instructed Moses to lead Israel there because he had determined one last humiliation for Pharaoh and the Egyptians, one last dramatic declaration of "I am the LORD" (Ex. 14:4) that would reverberate through human history.

But the Israelites didn't yet understand God's purposes, and when Pharaoh's army showed up, trapping them against the sea, they panicked and screamed to Moses, "Is it because there are no graves in Egypt that you have taken us away to die in the wilderness? What have you done to us in bringing us out of Egypt?" (Ex. 14:11).

They were trapped in a weak place. A place designed for them by God.

Moses replied to his terrified people, "Fear not, stand firm, and see the salvation of the LORD, which he will work for you today. For the Egyptians whom you see today, you shall never see again. The LORD will fight for you, and you have only to be silent" (Ex. 14:13–14). And fight for them he did. While holding off the Egyptian army with the pillar of fire, God opened for them a dry path through the sea. Then he let the Egyptians chase Israel hell-bent into the sea, which swallowed them. And on the other side of it all, Moses and the people erupted in a song we still sing today: "The LORD is my strength and my song, and he has become my salvation; this is my God, and I will praise him, my father's God, and I will exalt him" (Ex. 15:2).

Now, God could have made Israel a nation of Samsons. The Holy Spirit could have empowered them all to overcome Egypt with a bunch of donkey jaws. Why didn't God do that?

Well, remember Samson? After God gave Samson strength to overcome a thousand Philistines, what song did Samson sing? "With the jawbone of a donkey . . . have *I* struck down a thousand men" (Judg. 15:16). "*I* struck down." God may have been the source of Samson's strength, but since Samson didn't fully recognize it, God wasn't his song.

One reason God put Israel in that weak place is because he wanted them to know he was their strength and their salvation so that he would become their song.

And that's one reason he purposefully puts you in weak places. God is wise and faithful. He knows that we won't really understand what it means for him to be our strength and salvation until we find ourselves in a weak place where he is our only option. At first, it likely won't look or feel merciful, but later—sometimes much later—we realize how merciful it was. And then God really becomes our song.

PRAYER

Father, thank you for wisely, mercifully, and faithfully putting me in weak places so that I will learn that "when I am weak, then I am strong" (2 Cor. 12:10)—strong in the strength of your might. I want you to be my greatest strength because I want you to be my greatest song. In Jesus' name, amen.

MEDITATE MORE

Read Exodus 14:1–15:2. At what times in your life has God been your greatest song?

60

You make known to me the path of life; in your presence there is fullness of joy; at your right hand are pleasures forevermore.

PSALM 16:11

God Is Our Source of Satisfaction

GOD IS FAITHFUL . . . TO SHOW YOU THAT HE IS THE SOURCE OF ALL THAT SATISFIES

Our sun holds its planets in orbit with incomprehensible gravitational power and gives miraculous, abundant life to planet Earth. But what would happen if the Earth decided it no longer wished to orbit the sun, but launched off on its own course to seek its life from other sources? What if Earth believed that venerating Saturn really would unlock the secret to its soil's wealth-producing, future-securing fertility? What if it believed that the voluptuous eroticism of Venus would slake its craving? What if it believed the key to its joy was in wielding the scepter of power it thought Jupiter possessed? What would happen is that the sun-dependent life of Earth would die and all of Earth's pregnant hopes of finding satisfaction in Saturn (money), Venus (sex), and Jupiter (power) would be stillborn.

This is the fallen human condition. We have exchanged the sun for the empty promise of barren planets (Rom. 1:25).

> What's wrong with us at root [is] that instead of putting the worth of God on display with our money, sex, and power, we, by nature, actually make him disappear, as if the Creator and Sustainer of everything were inconsequential.[22]

It isn't that money, sex, and power are evils. In their proper orbits, they are glorious. But if we try to make these planets serve as our suns, they turn deadly. Our moral universe is thrown into destructive chaos and all our pursuits of sunlit happiness end in dark, barren misery.

> The Bible shows us another way. When the Son takes his glorious place at the center of the solar system of our lives, the massive pull of his

all-satisfying beauty corrects the erratic path of every planet, and makes the whole system sing with joy.[23]

God the Son is the faithful "sun of righteousness" (Mal. 4:2) who "gives life to the world" (John 6:33). Understanding this reality makes all reality understandable. And it allows "the heavens [to] declare the glory of God" (Ps. 19:1). The sun tells us of God. Its refrain in the heavenly oratory of God's glory is, God the Son is the "the light of the world" who gives us "the light of life" (John 8:12)! And "in [his] light do we see light" (Ps. 36:9)!

Hear the sun silently shout as its life-giving light floods and feeds the earth. Wealthy Saturn, erotic Venus, and powerful Jupiter are all glorious in their proper orbits, but barren and deadly as surrogate suns. God is the Sun of joy! Live in his light!

Jonathan Edwards said, "The enjoyment of God is the only happiness with which our souls can be satisfied."[24] Not only is this true, but only "in his presence"—enjoying him as the source—will all the lesser joys and pleasures God has made for us yield the fullness of satisfaction he designed them to bring us.

Restoring the divine Sun to his rightful place as our "exceeding joy" (Ps. 43:4) in the solar system of our lives is why Jesus came. For only in his presence is there fullness of joy; only at his right hand are there pleasures forevermore.

PRAYER

Father, thank you for mercifully and faithfully sending your Son to restore you, in your trinitarian fullness, as the sun of my world that I may experience the fullness of joy and pleasure in your presence, beginning now and in increasing measure forever. Deliver me from any temptation today to try and turn any "planet" you've created into a "sun." In Jesus' name, amen.

MEDITATE MORE

Read Luke 12:22–34. In this context, how is Jesus seeking to restore the divine Sun to his proper place as the source of all our joy?

61

Do not be anxious about anything, but in everything by prayer and supplication with thanksgiving let your requests be made known to God. And the peace of God, which surpasses all understanding, will guard your hearts and your minds in Christ Jesus. PHILIPPIANS 4:6–7

Resting on the Faithful One

GOD IS FAITHFUL . . . TO GIVE YOU PEACE IF YOU'LL RECEIVE IT

This famous text describes how faith works through prayer to release God's grace of peace in the life of a believer. But the peace Paul promises here will seem elusive to us if the focus of our faith is on the wrong thing.

Hudson Taylor, the great nineteenth-century missionary to China, struggled with this very issue. Here's how he described it:

> I strove for faith, but it would not come; I tried to exercise it, but in vain. Seeing more and more the wondrous supply of grace laid up in Jesus, the fullness of our precious Saviour, my guilt and helplessness seemed to increase. Sins committed appeared but as trifles compared with the sin of unbelief which was their cause, which could not or would not take God at His word, but rather made Him a liar! Unbelief was, I felt, the damning sin of the world; yet I indulged in it. I prayed for faith, but it came not. What was I to do?[25]

Then he experienced a breakthrough that changed his life:

> When my agony of soul was at its height, a sentence in a letter from [John] McCarthy was used to remove the scales from my eyes. . . . "But how to get faith strengthened? Not by striving after faith, but by resting on the Faithful One." As I read, I saw it all! "If we believe not, he abideth faithful." I looked to Jesus and saw (and when I saw, oh, how joy flowed!) that He had said, "I will never leave thee." "Ah, *there* is rest!" I thought. "I have striven in vain to rest in Him. I'll strive no more."[26]

The key for Taylor was that he stopped focusing on trying to exercise more faith. Instead, he looked to Jesus, "the Faithful One," as revealed in the written word. While his focus had been on his lack of faith and trying to work it up, he was miserable. But when his focus turned to the fullness of Jesus, he discovered the peace surpassing understanding.

Faith is not a muscle we need to build up in order to be strong enough to trust Jesus. Faith is "resting on" Jesus as "the Faithful One" because faith is our response to seeing Jesus as strong enough to bear our anxious burdens and meet our needs. The more trustworthy, solid, stable, dependable, unfailing, and secure he appears to us, the more we will rest on him, and therefore the stronger our faith in him will be.

When our faith is weak, it's an indicator that our focus is likely on the wrong thing, inhibiting us from resting on him. Faith is not faith in our faith in Jesus. It is faith *in Jesus*.

He said, "My peace I give to you" (John 14:27). It's ours for the taking. All we need to do is ask in faith in everything. And the faith-key that unlocks the peace that surpasses understanding is resting on him as the Faithful One, trusting in his ability to do what he has promised.

PRAYER

Father, thank you for making faith not something I must work up, but a resting on you and your faithful Son to carry my burdens and meet my needs. This helps me understand what Jesus meant when he invited me to come to him to find rest for my soul (Matt. 11:28–29). Give me grace to see him more clearly that I may rest more profoundly on him. In Jesus' name, amen.

MEDITATE MORE

Review Matthew 11:28–29 so, in light of this meditation, you may more profoundly take hold of the promise of Philippians 4:6–7.

You Don't Have
to Know God's Will

GOD IS FAITHFUL . . . WHEN HE DOESN'T ANSWER YOUR
SPECIFIC QUESTIONS ABOUT HIS WILL

When we're seeking God's will, we often want to know specifically what we're supposed to do, where we're supposed to go, how our needs will be provided, or why the terrible thing happened. What we're seeking is certainty because we believe certainty gives us peace. But God knows the answers we think we want would rarely provide us the peace we seek because we lack the omniscient perspective it requires to make sense of them. That's why Hudson Taylor counsels us,

> Make up your mind that God is an infinite Sovereign, and has the right to do as He pleases with His own, and He may not explain to you a thousand things which may puzzle your reason in His dealings with you.[27]

Our "infinite Sovereign" knows that our fundamental need is to learn to trust him over our very finite understanding (Prov. 3:5). He knows that trust will provide us what explanations won't: the peace that surpasses understanding (Phil. 4:7).

That's why when we pray to know God's will, God's answers address our need to trust in him more than the understanding we think we need. Therefore, we can fail to recognize his answers at first, and mistake them for God not providing the peace we need. But God promises that we will experience peace through *believing* (Rom. 15:13). Believing what? Believing his "precious and very great promises" (2 Peter 1:4).

God's promises are the checks that are accepted at the bank of heaven.

They are God's promissory notes to us, guaranteeing that he will make good on the value they represent. That's why Charles Spurgeon said,

> When I pray, I like to go to God just as I go to a bank clerk when I have [a] cheque to be cashed. I walk in, put the cheque down on the counter, and the clerk gives me my money, I take it up, and go about my business.[28]

This might sound simplistic, but it's not. It's simple faith in the profound promises of a God who omnisciently upholds every aspect of the unfathomably complex universe "by the word of his power" (Heb. 1:3). Trusting in his promises to have the certainty that produces the peace we need is eminently reasonable. Trusting in our understanding to experience peace-giving certainty is not.

There are times God does give us specific answers regarding his will for us, and it's not wrong to ask. But overall, living in the will of God is more about knowing and trusting God's specific promises to us than receiving his specific direction (Heb. 11:8). It's more about resting in his sovereignty than wrestling over our ambiguity (Ps. 131:1–2).

When we face confounding questions or situations, hear Jesus' counsel: "Let not your hearts be troubled. Believe in God; believe also in me" (John 14:1). You don't have to know God's will if you are confident in God's word. For God's will is to faithfully say yes in Christ to every promise he makes to us in Scripture (2 Cor. 1:20). And God's word is as good as God.

PRAYER

Father, thank you for every time you mercifully and faithfully did not give a specific answer to my request to know your will, since you are all-wise and all-knowing, and I am not. When my heart becomes troubled over some question regarding your will, help me remember that peace is found in believing in your promises to me and not in specifically understanding how you plan to answer them. In Jesus' name, amen.

MEDITATE MORE

Read John 14:1–14, and know how Jesus answered his troubled disciples' specific questions.

63

I have learned in whatever situation I am to be content.... I can do all things through him who strengthens me.

PHILIPPIANS 4:11, 13

The End of Your Discontentment

God Is Faithful ... to Direct You to Seek Your Contentment in Him

Once upon a time, the king and queen of the living lived contented in the garden of God. They had everything they needed, and so they did not need much. They walked every day with their Creator, and he infused their every moment and movement with meaning. They loved and trusted him perfectly. They did not live by fruit alone but on every word that proceeded from the mouth of God.

Then came a fateful day when they chose to eat the one fruit forbidden by the mouth of God. They believed there was more life in the fruit than in the word of life. But there was death in the fruit. The contentment they sought in the fruit died as they ate, and the fairy tale turned into a nightmare.

But though the fallen king and queen ceased their faithful perfection, their perfect Creator remained faithful and, in love, immediately set into motion the eucatastrophe of redemption that would undo the catastrophe they had brought upon themselves and all their descendants.[29] For any willing to trust him fully again, the Creator would himself bear the just punishment he had pronounced upon them and restore to them perfection, immortality, and all the contentment in him they could possibly contain.

And as a great mercy to them, as long as they remained in their fallen state, he made their curse-induced unquenchable discontentment a constant reminder that contentment does exist and a pointer to where it is found.

* * *

My fairy-tale telling of humanity's fall and redemption illustrates that there is an end—both a purpose and a termination—of your discontentment. It is a mercifully frustrating, chronic, daily reminder that the fruit on the trees of the world can never replace God. They cannot because they were never meant to. C. S. Lewis said it beautifully:

If I find in myself a desire which no experience in this world can satisfy, the most probable explanation is that I was made for another world. If none of my earthly pleasures satisfy it, that does not prove that the universe is a fraud. Probably earthly pleasures were never meant to satisfy it, but only to arouse it, to suggest the real thing.[30]

This profound insight not only helps us understand the role of earthly pleasures, but also the only way earthly pleasures can really be enjoyed: for Christians, as tangible expressions of God's goodness, when enjoyed as he designed them; for non-Christians, as pointers to God's existence and goodness.

That's why Paul exhorts us not "to set [our] hopes on the uncertainty of riches, but on God, who richly provides us with everything to enjoy" (1 Tim. 6:17). And it's also why, writing from prison, he was able to say, "I have learned in whatever situation I am to be content. . . . I can do all things through him who strengthens me" (Phil. 4:11, 13).

When you really believe that God is the true source of your contentment, you become free from seeking it in the fruit of the trees of the world. You can find it anywhere your faithful Creator places you. And you discover that, like the pre-fall Adam and Eve, you do not need much.

PRAYER

Father, thank you that there is an end—both a purpose and a termination—to my unquenchable discontentment. And for faithfully showing me that you are that ultimate end. Whatever it takes, free me from any residual unbelief that leads me to faithlessly seek contentment in the fruit of the trees of the world, but to enjoy them, according to your intended design, as manifestations of your goodness. In Jesus' name, amen.

MEDITATE MORE

Read Philippians 4:10–13. To what degree have you learned the secret of being content in *any* situation?

How Can We Be Angry and Not Sin?

GOD IS FAITHFUL . . . TO TEACH YOU HOW TO BE RIGHTEOUSLY ANGRY

Is this even possible? Not if perfect, sinless anger is the requirement, since sin infects everything we think, say, and do. But Paul wasn't referring to perfect, sinless anger here, but anger rooted in the prideful, selfish soil of our sin nature.

So, what is righteous anger? Since what God says (Heb. 6:5) and what God does (Mic. 6:8) are good because they are "righteous altogether" (Ps. 19:9), righteous anger is being angry at what makes God angry, because God's anger is an expression of his righteousness. And what makes God angry is the perversion of his goodness; the turning wrong of what he made right. God calls this perversion *evil* because it profanes his glory and distorts reality, resulting in the destruction of joy for every creature who chooses the evil perversion over God's good.

God's righteousness demands his anger over such destructive perversion and that he mete out commensurate justice against those who commit such evil.

What is sinful anger? It's anger springing from our sinful selfishness. It's when we feel more anger over an offense to our pride than the marring of God's glory, more anger over a minor inconvenience than a grievous injustice. It's anger that produces "quarreling, jealousy, anger, hostility, slander, gossip, conceit, and disorder" (2 Cor. 12:20). This "anger of man does not produce the righteousness of God" (James 1:20).

Righteous anger doesn't look or feel like sinful anger because godly righteous anger is governed and directed by love. God describes himself as "merciful and gracious, slow to anger, and abounding in steadfast love and faithfulness" (Ex. 34:6). Though God will eventually bring his righteous judgment to bear on the unrepentant guilty (Ex. 34:7), he "does not afflict from his heart" (Lam. 3:33). He does "not [wish] that any should perish, but that all should reach repentance" (2 Peter 3:9).

If you want to see faithful, love-governed anger, look at Jesus. He, of course, knew a day of judgment was coming when he would tread his enemies in "the winepress of the fury of the wrath of God" (Rev. 19:15). But long before bringing judgment, he came to bring salvation to his enemies (John 12:47). And when he came to save, he rarely expressed anger.

Therefore, like him, we are to be "quick to hear, slow to speak, slow to anger" (James 1:19). There are times we must get angry, but, like Jesus, our anger must be laced with grief (Mark 3:5). Sometimes we must flip over tables (John 2:15–17), but we must also weep over what made this necessary (Luke 13:34).

Righteous anger is roused by evil that profanes God's holiness and perverts his goodness. But it's also governed by God's love and therefore slow to be expressed, first pursuing redemptive acts of love if at all possible.

We will never be perfectly angry in this age. But as we seek to be conformed to the image of Christ (Rom. 8:29), God is faithful to teach us how to be righteously angry and not sinfully angry.

PRAYER

Father, forgive me for too often indulging sinful, selfish anger, and too often failing to be righteously angry over things about which I should. Help me today to grow in the grace of being like you: slow to anger and abounding in steadfast love and faithfulness. And when anger is appropriate, to be angry and not sin. In Jesus' name, amen.

MEDITATE MORE

Read James 1:19. How can you apply these three exhortations today?

65

"It is better for me to die than to live." But God said to Jonah, "Do you do well to be angry for the plant?" And he said, "Yes, I do well to be angry, angry enough to die." JONAH 4:8-9

God's Mercy When We're Caught in Self-Pity

GOD IS FAITHFUL . . . TO CONFRONT OUR SELF-PITY WITH HIS KINDNESS

Jonah's plant had died, the one that gave him shade. God had sent the worm that killed it. And Jonah was so mad he just wanted to die. God, with his question, mirrored back Jonah's disproportionate anger. *Really? You're angry about the plant?* Jonah doubled down.

We recognize Jonah's frame of mind because we've all been there. We've all said things just as ridiculous in anger—the anger of self-pity. Jonah's anger wasn't primarily about the plant; the plant was just the last straw. Jonah was angry over Nineveh.

Actually, Jonah was angry with God and what God had decided *not to do* to that Assyrian capital city, even though the Assyrians had done such brutal things to Israel. God had instructed the prophet to prophesy God's impending judgment to the citizens of Nineveh, and Jonah hadn't wanted to go. He feared the Ninevites might take it to heart and repent, and that God, being merciful, would relent his judgment and the Assyrians would get away with murder. And sure enough, they repented and God relented.

I don't wish to unfairly reduce Jonah's response to *mere* self-pity. If we had been in his shoes, we too likely would have found God's grace toward the Assyrian leaders and people hard to comprehend. By any historical standard, they were unfathomably cruel to peoples they conquered. Imagine it being 1944, and observing revival break out in Berlin, with Hitler leading his Third Reich in repenting for their terrible atrocities and God extending them mercy. Would we feel justice had been done?

But self-pity is clearly present in Jonah. Self-pity is our faithless, pride-fueled response to something not going the way we think it should. We often don't recognize it—or don't want to recognize it—right away because we feel justified in indulging it after the injustice we believe we've suffered. A dead giveaway is how closed we are to receiving anyone else's perspective—even God's—that brings a correction to ours.

As Jonah saw it, God had given him a message he didn't want to preach, then God dramatically opposed his effort to get out of his assignment by escaping to Tarshish, then God gave the Assyrians mercy they certainly didn't deserve, and then, to top it off, God killed the plant that gave Jonah the one small comfort he enjoyed in all his misery. It all felt so unjust. And in the bitter anger of self-pity, which we all recognize, Jonah lashed out at God and told him he'd rather be dead.

But in God's response to Jonah, we see his faithfulness and mercy:

> "You pity [are more upset over] the plant, for which you did not labor, nor did you make it grow, which came into being in a night and perished in a night. And should not I pity Nineveh, that great city, in which there are more than 120,000 persons who do not know their right hand from their left, and also much cattle?" (Jonah 4:10–11)

This was a rebuke, but a kind one. God knew Jonah's frame, remembering he was dust (Ps. 103:14). God knew there was real confusion and pain woven with Jonah's sinful self-pity, as there often is with ours. So, he sought to lead Jonah to repentance with kindness (Rom. 2:4) by confronting his self-pity with his true, gracious perspective: Assyrians too were sinners whose terrible sin he could justly cover if they also repented.

This is often how God faithfully pursues us in our sinful self-pity, and often the best approach we can take with others in theirs.

PRAYER

Father, thank you for how you kindly and faithfully pursued Jonah in his self-pity, and for the many times you have kindly led me to repentance when I have been caught in this sin. In Jesus' name, amen.

MEDITATE MORE

Read Jonah 4 and consider what has been most effective in freeing you from the grip of self-pity.

66

"Therefore do not be anxious about tomorrow, for tomorrow will be anxious for itself. Sufficient for the day is its own trouble."

MATTHEW 6:34

Today's Grace Is for Today's Troubles

GOD IS FAITHFUL . . . TO CARRY OUR ANXIETIES OVER TOMORROW'S TROUBLES

In this command, Jesus is offering us his easy yoke (Matt. 11:30). Anxiety over our uncertain, and as yet unreal, future is a heavy burden, one he doesn't want us to bear. Because we're not designed to bear it. The future is God's burden, and for him it's very light.

But Satan and our sinful unbelief encourage us to focus on the future—not the real future as defined by God's foreknowledge and promises, but an imaginary future as defined by our fears. When we allow our anxiety about an imagined tomorrow to govern us, it distracts our attention from the only place God's grace is available to us: today, right now, in the real world. It inhibits us from seeking first the kingdom of God in reality (Matt. 6:33) because we feel compelled to seek first our temporal security in the unreal future. But as John Piper says, "Tomorrow's troubles are not designed to be dealt with by today's grace."[31]

That's why Jesus wants us focused on *today*. Because the grace God provides us today is designed to be completely sufficient for today's troubles (2 Cor. 9:8). By commanding us to "not be anxious about tomorrow," Jesus is inviting us to lay aside the weight of tomorrow's trouble by exercising two simple acts of faith: *casting* and *receiving*.

We are to *cast* our anxieties for tomorrow on God because he cares for us (1 Peter 5:7). Our fears for the future are immensely unreliable, so we're foolish if we allow them to govern us. We don't know the future, and neither does Satan—and he wouldn't tell us the truth even if he did know (John 8:44). But God completely knows the future (Isa. 46:10), so we are wise to trust him with ours. We cast our cares on him by bringing our requests to him, leaving them with him, and allowing his peace to guard our hearts and minds (Phil. 4:6–7).

Then we are to *receive* from God his sufficient grace for today. His grace doesn't always come in the packages we expect. Sometimes his grace looks like abundance and sometimes it looks like need (Phil. 4:12). But God promises that his grace is sufficient in prosperity and affliction, in rejoicing and weeping, in freedom and imprisonment, in life and in death. His grace looks different in each situation, but God will always provide enough grace for what we really need so we "can do all things through him who strengthens" us (Phil. 4:13).

"Sufficient for the day is its own trouble" (Matt. 6:34). And sufficient for today is today's grace. Today's grace won't address tomorrow's troubles, except for today's grace to help us cast today's anxieties about tomorrow on God. And this easy yoke from Jesus is a wonderful gift. Because it frees us from distracting, demanding imaginary fears of an unreal future, so we can focus on the one real place we can actually experience God's faithful provision of the grace we need: *today*.

PRAYER

Father, thank you for the precious and very great promise you made to me through Jesus: that if I seek the kingdom first, all that I need will be added to me (Matt. 6:33). Grant me today's allotment of grace for today's allotment of troubles, including the grace to cast on you any troubling anxieties I experience today over tomorrow's troubles. In Jesus' name, amen.

MEDITATE MORE

Read Matthew 6:19–34. How does our fear for tomorrow kill our faith for today?

67

The LORD God called to the man and said to him, "Where are you?" And he said, "I heard the sound of you in the garden, and I was afraid, because I was naked, and I hid myself." GENESIS 3:9-10

Your One Refuge from Your Shame

GOD IS FAITHFUL . . . TO TRANSFORM YOUR SHAME INTO A STORY OF HIS POWERFUL GRACE

Her life had become a moral train wreck, so she came to the well when the sun blazed hot to hide from the comments, whispers, condemning looks, and non-looks (John 4). He had shamefully abused his great power, impregnated another man's wife, and arranged a murderous cover-up to hide his wickedness (2 Sam. 11). She had come to Jesus for healing from a vaginal hemorrhage she'd suffered for twelve long years, but to keep her culturally shameful bodily weakness hidden, she just secretly touched the fringe of his robe (Luke 8:43–48).

The woman at the well, King David, and the hemorrhaging woman are three biblical portraits of people who, for different reasons, tried to hide their shame. But when each encountered God and experienced his power to remove their shame, they discovered they had sought to hide in the wrong places.

As our text illustrates, shame has plagued us since Adam and Eve ate the fruit, became ashamed of their nakedness, grew fearful of God and each other, and began to hide. And no wonder. Their sin exposed them to God's righteous judgment (Gen. 3:17–19; Rom. 6:23), other sinners' sinful judgment and rejection, and to the condemning accusations of the evil one (Rev. 12:10). They'd become damaged, vulnerable people with an evil streak, living in a dangerous world. And we're just like them.

It's not that our desire to seek refuge from the effects of our shameful sins and weaknesses is wrong. But the refuges we choose often are. For there's only one hiding place that offers the protection we seek, where all our shame is not only covered but transformed and we no longer need to fear: the refuge

God provides, which we now know is Jesus (Heb. 6:18–20).

Only in Jesus' substitutionary death for us is there full, just atonement for and complete cleansing from our shameful sins (Acts 4:12; 1 John 1:9). And only God's powerful grace that flows to us through Jesus is so sufficient that it can transform our once-shameful weaknesses into such strengths that they give us cause to boast in Christ's power (2 Cor. 12:9–10). Sin-fueled shame declares us guilty. Jesus, our righteousness (Phil. 3:9), pronounces us guiltless. Weakness-fueled shame declares us deficient. Jesus, our strength, declares that his strong grace will be sufficient for us in all our weaknesses, which was God's design for us from the beginning.

God is the only truly safe refuge from the effects of our shameful sins and weaknesses. That's what the woman at the well discovered: Jesus transformed the life she was ashamed of into such a compelling testimony of grace and hope that "many Samaritans from [her] town believed in him" (John 4:39). That's what King David discovered: his story of God's amazing grace of forgiveness has taught millions of "transgressors [God's] ways," and moved countless "sinners [to] return to" God (Ps. 51:13). And that's what the hemorrhaging woman discovered: Jesus did expose her shameful weakness, and then transformed it into a showcase of his all-sufficient grace in which she could boast (Luke 8:48).

And since we're just like them, Jesus will faithfully do this for us too, if, in our shame, we make him our hiding place.

PRAYER

Father, thank you for your powerful sin-destroying, weakness-transforming grace that breaks the power of my shame if I come to you for refuge. I do come! And remind me every time I feel shame that you are always faithful to free me from condemnation if I make you my hiding place. In Jesus' name, amen.

MEDITATE MORE

Read John 4, 2 Samuel 11–12, and Luke 8:43–48 to soak in God's shame-destroying grace that's available to you in Jesus.

68

Why are you cast down, O my soul, and why are you in turmoil within me? Hope in God; for I shall again praise him, my salvation and my God. PSALM 42:11

What Your Moods Are Telling You

GOD IS FAITHFUL . . . TO HELP YOU SEE WHERE
YOU ARE PLACING YOUR HOPE

Psalm 42 was inspired by a bad mood David was experiencing. And just these two sentences provide us a helpful, simple model for addressing our bad moods.

If calling David's experience a "mood" seems to trivialize it, it's probably because we've learned to think wrongly about moods from our culture. People commonly think of moods as emotional weather patterns; they blow in and eventually blow over. If we get caught in a bad mood, we just need to wait till it passes. If others are affected, we tell them, "I'm just in a bad mood." But moods don't just happen to us, like the weather. They tell us important things we need to know.

If our bodies are functioning normally, our moods often spring from something we're *believing,* truths or lies influencing us at the time. This is God's design. He created us to be governed not by mere instincts, but by what we believe—he designed us to live by faith. And he integrated our souls and bodies in such a way that what we functionally believe at any given time manifests as our *emotional frame of mind,* which is what we call "moods."

This means moods frequently function as *belief gauges,* indicators that tell us what's currently fueling or syphoning away our hope. When we're in a bad mood—an emotional frame of mind we don't have a godly, faithful reason to be in—that mood may be informing us that something isn't right in the belief department, so we will examine what's going on and make adjustments if necessary.

This is what we see David doing in our two-sentence text above. First, he queried himself: "Why are you cast down, O my soul, and why are you in turmoil within me?"

This is an important question to ask our moods, because they aren't always *belief gauges*; they can also be *body chemistry gauges*, indicating something is affecting or infecting our body—sickness, disease, mental illness—and their treatments are well-known mood influencers, as are certain hormonal imbalances. Rigorous exercise, sleep deprivation, chronic pain, caffeine, sugar, and illicit drugs can all alter our body chemistry and affect our moods. So, we need to ask ourselves, "Why am I feeling this way?" because moods are important indicators.

In David's case, his mood turned out to be a belief gauge. His situation appeared grim, leading him to *believe* there was little hope of a good outcome. This belief emotionally manifested in his depressed *mood* ("cast down"). His depressed mood indicated he needed to take action to address his hope deficit.

So that's what he did. David didn't passively wait for his mood to blow over; instead, he exhorted—preached to—his soul to "hope in God." In other words, "Soul, you're losing hope because of how dire your circumstances appear. Stop it! Remember what God has promised you, remember that he's faithful, and hope in him!"

We aren't victims of our bad moods, like we are of bad weather; we're beneficiaries of our bad moods. As body chemistry gauges, they tell us if something's off or wrong with our health. As belief gauges, they tell us if something's wrong with what we're believing. And in both cases, these moods are expressions of God's mercy and faithfulness to direct us once again to the one source of all our hope: *in him.*

PRAYER

Father, thank you for designing my moods as gauges of my belief health, or gauges of my bodily health, which also affects my beliefs. Help me pay greater attention to what they are telling me today. In Jesus' name, amen.

MEDITATE MORE

Read Psalms 42 and 43 (they originally were one psalm) and observe how David uses both his emotional frame of mind and God's promises to fight for hope.

69

A man who flatters his neighbor spreads a net for his feet.

PROVERBS 29:5

When You're Tempted to Flatter Someone

GOD IS FAITHFUL . . . TO WARN YOU OF THE DANGERS OF FLATTERY

A good illustration of this proverb comes from this interaction between Jesus and some Pharisees:

> "Teacher, we know that you are true and do not care about anyone's opinion. For you are not swayed by appearances, but truly teach the way of God. Is it lawful to pay taxes to Caesar, or not? Should we pay them, or should we not?" But, knowing their hypocrisy, he said to them, "Why put me to the test?" (Mark 12:14–15)

Flattery is a form of deception. It sounds so much like respect and graciousness, but the speaker's motive is not to give grace to the person to whom it's addressed but to manipulate them for the benefit of the speaker.

We learn early that flattery can grease the wheels of obtaining something we want, whether it's to enhance our standing in the eyes of someone who might benefit us socially or financially, or to conceal our dishonest dealings with someone, or to discredit, perhaps destroy, another's reputation or influence. And a speaker and hearer can both be guilty of flattery when both know what's going on, and the damage being done is to a third party.

God calls us to speak "the truth in love" (Eph. 4:15), because the truth is a faithful representation of what is real. And speaking the truth in love means delivering a true word for the purpose of giving "grace to those who hear" (Eph. 4:29).

But the truth that gives the kind of grace hearers really need is not always a soothing truth to hear. Sometimes we're called to give grace to someone in the form of a reproof or rebuke (2 Tim. 4:2). And that's when we must remember that "whoever rebukes a man will afterward find more favor than he who flatters with his tongue" (Prov. 28:23).

Flattery is contrasted with a rebuke in this proverb because it highlights whose benefit the speaker is seeking—and there's a heaven-and-hell difference between the two. A rebuke is truth that's not only harder to hear than flattery, it's usually truth a speaker is reluctant to deliver, but does so out of a loving desire to see a hearer benefit from the grace of God. That's why love never flatters, and wisdom never desires to be flattered.

But sin is neither loving nor wise. Which means there's part of us (our indwelling sin) that is easily tempted to manipulate others with flattery for our own benefit, as well as enjoys being flattered. It is a seductive temptation because the short-term reward can appear appealing. But because it's a form of lying, it will eventually wreak destruction.

In this case of the Pharisees, they employed flattery in an attempt to snare Jesus into a no-win situation: either anger the Romans or anger the crowd. The Pharisees knew better; they likely had the book of Proverbs memorized. But Jesus discerned their hypocrisy and didn't fall for their trap. And if they never repented, the destruction it wreaked was their own.

Jesus is always faithful to speak the truth we most need to hear from the greatest love we can receive. Sometimes his loving truth is hard to hear, but he only speaks it because he wants to give us grace. And he calls us to do the same with one another, and never to lay a deceptive net for our neighbor's feet.

PRAYER

Father, thank you for your Son who speaks the truth in love, because he is the truth you spoke in love. Give me grace today to give grace to those who hear me and to deliver me from any temptation to use flattery. In Jesus' name, amen.

MEDITATE MORE

Read Mark 12:13–17. What grace do you receive from Jesus' words, "Render to Caesar the things that are Caesar's, and to God the things that are God's" (v. 17)?

70

Flee from sexual immorality. . . . You are not your own, for you were bought with a price. So glorify God in your body.

1 CORINTHIANS 6:18–20

The Real Root of Sexual Sin

GOD IS FAITHFUL . . . TO FREE YOU FROM ENSLAVEMENT TO SEXUAL IMMORALITY

What does the Bible diagnose as the root of human sexual perversion—what we often and rightly call sexual brokenness? We can see it clearly in Romans 1:24–26: "Therefore God gave them up in the lusts of their hearts to impurity, to the dishonoring of their bodies among themselves, because they exchanged the truth about God for a lie and worshiped and served the creature rather than the Creator."

"The dishonoring of their bodies," which refers to sexual sin in all its deviant heterosexual, homosexual, and other expressions, is a manifestation of humanity unhinged from its Creator. It's just one fruit, human pride.

Pride is a black hole of consuming selfishness at the core of fallen human nature. Pride's nature is to consume, to bring all things into the self. It sees other people, the created world, and God himself as objects to use in service to one's self-oriented desires.

So just as gluttony or anorexia is pride infecting and manipulating the self's orientation toward food, or greed is pride infecting and manipulating the self's orientation toward money, sexual immorality is pride infecting and manipulating the self's orientation toward sex.

But when Paul says God gives up a people "in the lusts of their hearts to impurity," he's mainly (though not exclusively) referring to a corporate judgment. God removes the societal restraints on the sexual expressions of pride, resulting in a collective slide into consuming sexual destruction. So, we must keep in mind that our biggest personal and corporate problem is not sex; it's pride.

Therefore, our most powerful weapon in the fight against sexual impurity is a profound humility. And humility is a deep realization and embrace of the truth that we are not our own.

This is why Paul said what he did to the Corinthians in our opening text. Yes, "flee[ing] from sexual immorality"—taking behavioral action—is necessary. But notice that Paul's primary emphasis is not on behavior modification or deliverance from demonic oppression, both of which are realities of our complex human experience and so have a place in our fight for sexual purity. However, Paul sees the primary issue in our sexual struggle as addressing the remaining pride within us.

That's why the key to our freedom, the great tamer of our sexual sin, is in our embracing this reality: "I have been crucified with Christ. It is no longer I who live, but Christ who lives in me. And the life I now live in the flesh I live by faith in the Son of God, who loved me and gave himself for me" (Gal. 2:20).

This is what it means that we are "not our own." This is the powerful grace of humility God has faithfully and mercifully provided us that breaks the enslaving power of pride infecting our sinful sexual desires. For true freedom is not the liberty to freely express our pride-fueled sexual desires—true freedom is found in the humble belief that we are "not our own." This is what frees us from our slavery to our all-consuming pride to be what God created us to be.

PRAYER

Father, thank you for providing, through Jesus, not only everything I need to be cleansed from the guilt of my sexual sin but also the power to overcome the pride that fuels it. In any sexual temptation I may face today, help me remember that I am not my own, that you have bought me with a price and, if I trust you, you will provide me the powerful grace to glorify you with my body. In Jesus' name, amen.

MEDITATE MORE

Read Romans 6:1–14 to remind you how to keep sin from "reign[ing] in your mortal body, to make you obey its passions" (v. 12).

How Not to Be Anxious about Your Life

GOD IS FAITHFUL . . . TO EMPOWER YOU TO OBEY HIS HUMANLY IMPOSSIBLE COMMAND

Anxiety is a species of fear. It's the paralyzing fear that something we dread might possibly come true. And there's only one solution to anxiety: the assurance everything is going to be okay.

But the world gives us no such assurances. We find ourselves surrounded by myriad real dangers resulting in an endless list of "what if" fears. It's no wonder human beings are so afflicted with anxiety. This makes Jesus' command to "not be anxious" seemingly impossible to obey. And it is as if we're on our own to obey it. But as Jesus says, "With man it is impossible, but not with God. For all things are possible with God" (Mark 10:27).

That's why God the Son entered this dangerous, demonic world, where even man's greatest efforts to ensure safety are ultimately and decidedly defeated by death. And when he did, he made the most audacious claim ever uttered by human lips: "that whoever believes in him should not perish but have eternal life" (John 3:16). For that person, everything is going to be ultimately, gloriously, wonderfully okay. Then to demonstrate the reality of his claim and therefore its trustworthiness, he decidedly defeated death and announced "all authority in heaven and on earth" had been given to him (Matt. 28:18).

It is with this authority he says to us, "Do not be anxious about your life." Jesus has made himself the antidote to our anxiety. What he accomplished for us and promises to us is the ultimate triumph over all that terrifies us. Although he does not promise us escape from misery in this world, he does promise to redeem every misery and work it for our ultimate good (Rom. 8:28), and that in him we will overcome the worst the world can do to us (Rom. 8:35–39).

Yes, he is commanding us to believe what is impossible—with man. But this should not surprise us. Jesus commands us to believe that "everyone who lives and believes in [him] shall never die" (John 11:26). Jesus commands us to love one another *just like he has loved us* (John 15:12). Jesus commands us to renounce all we have (Luke 14:33), because we are more confident in the treasures we have in heaven (Mark 10:21). Most of Jesus' commands are impossible for mere humans. But they're not impossible "with God."

God faithfully empowers us to obey this command if, "by prayer and supplication with thanksgiving," we make our "requests . . . known to God," trust a specific promise he's made us, receive his "peace . . . which surpasses all understanding" (Phil. 4:6–7), and cease to be anxious in the strength he supplies (1 Peter 4:11).

Therefore, Jesus says to you, right now, right where you are, "Do not be anxious about your life." He says this knowing all that's in your past, your temperament, the seriousness of your current crises, and how intensely you fear the possible threats you dread. Because if you believe in him, he will be faithful to his promise that for you, everything is going to be ultimately, gloriously, eternally, inexpressibly wonderfully okay. For with him, all things are possible.

PRAYER

Father, I confess that on my own it is impossible for me not to be anxious about my life. But I also confess that with you, all things are possible. Therefore, help me cast my anxieties on you today that I may cease to be anxious in the strength you promise to supply me through Christ, in whose name I pray, amen.

MEDITATE MORE

Review Luke 12:22–34 to remind yourself that "it is your Father's good pleasure to give you the kingdom" (v. 32).

72

When my anxious thoughts multiply within me, your comfort delights my soul. PSALM 94:19 NASB

Don't Talk to Your Anxiety, Talk to God

GOD IS FAITHFUL ... TO GIVE YOU PEACE IF YOU GIVE HIM YOUR FEARS

Your anxieties talk to you. They're demanding, insistent, argumentative, and inconsolable. Don't talk back to them. Talk to God.

This can be hard because anxieties often disguise themselves in our imaginations. They present scenarios that appear emotionally compelling to dwell upon. Anxieties can even impersonate, taking the form of people—often people we know. These are particularly insidious.

In real life, these people might be family members, friends, fellow church members, coworkers, acquaintances, or people we only know by reputation. They might be people with whom we disagree or have a relational strain. They might be people we fear disappointing, or fear confronting with a hard truth, or whose influence we fear might damage our loved one or our church. Or they might just be people whose righteous lives reflect negatively on our failings.

Whoever they *really* are, our anxiety comes to us in our imagination disguised as that person saying provocative things, and we reply. Before we know it, we have engaged in a lengthy fantasy argument that does nothing but enflame our faithless anxiety and indulge a false sense of self-justification, while also unjustly arousing uncharitable emotions toward the real person. When we talk to our anxieties, our "anxious thoughts multiply within" us, and often so do other sins.

God never instructs us in Scripture to fight anxiety by arguing with it. It almost never works. Scripture only instructs us to cast our anxieties on God in prayer and trust him to meet our needs, whatever they are (1 Peter 5:7; Phil. 4:19).

I'm not saying all anxiety is sinful, because the Bible doesn't say this. Jesus sinlessly experienced anxiety in Gethsemane (Matt. 26:38–39) and Paul had "daily . . . anxiety for all the churches" he planted (2 Cor. 11:28). Christian parents should feel some anxiety over the spiritually dangerous influences their children face, as should Christian citizens over the progression of cultural and institutionalized evil in their nation. The Bible gives us warrant to feel anxious concern over the real or potential destructive effects of evil on precious souls.

What keeps these anxieties from turning sinful is when, like Jesus and Paul, we translate our fear-fueled concerns into prayer requests, weaving them with thanksgiving for past graces we've received from God and the future graces he's promised us (2 Peter 1:4), and then give them over to God. When this occurs, a spiritually beautiful exchange takes place: God receives glory as the all-sufficient, abundantly generous object of our faith (2 Cor. 9:8), and like the psalmist, we can say that God's "comfort delights my soul." He guards our minds and hearts with peace that surpasses our understanding through faith (Phil. 4:6–7).

As long as we live in this fallen world, we're going to experience anxieties. Some are legitimate, others aren't. But beware of listening to what your anxieties tell you. And don't talk back to them, especially anxieties disguised as someone else in your imagination. Prayer is God's faithful provision for dealing with all our anxieties. Talk to God and cast all your "what if" concerns on him because only he can give you the assurance that everything is going to be ultimately, gloriously, eternally, inexpressibly wonderfully okay.

PRAYER

Father, forgive me for every time I've faithlessly enflamed my anxieties by mentally indulging them, and especially when I've wronged others by using them to embody my anxieties in my imagination. Today, help me remember to tell my anxieties to you so I will receive the peace I really need. In Jesus' name, amen.

MEDITATE MORE

Review Philippians 4:6–7. Repeat it ten times and take it with you as a reminder when you are tempted.

73

"Whoever would be great among you must be your servant, and whoever would be first among you must be slave of all. For even the Son of Man came not to be served but to serve, and to give his life as a ransom for many." MARK 10:43–45

Jesus Can Free You from a Burdensome Self-Image

GOD IS FAITHFUL . . . TO SHOW YOU THE PATH TO TRUE GREATNESS

I have a long list of inadequacies I frequently feel: how little I've read, how slow I write, my gaps in good parenting, my paralysis in certain kinds of decision-making, my concentration struggles, my continual vulnerability to old sinful patterns . . . I could go on and on. You probably can sympathize with me, because of your own long list.

Our cumulative sense of inadequacy might feel like a low self-image, but its roots are often in thinking more highly of ourselves than we ought to think and wanting others to admire us more than we deserve. Our shame is often due to an exaggeratedly high self-image we feel entitled to, which makes living with and trying to address our limitations, weaknesses, and sins more burdensome than necessary.

Which is why Jesus' statement here in Mark 10 is a paradoxical message of liberation for us. If we want to be great, we "must be slave of all." That's quintessentially Jesus: what we associate with bondage is the path to freedom; what we associate with greatness is the path to bondage. But he's right, and our experience bears it out.

The greatest tyrant known to humanity is the sinful, pathologically selfish, self-exalting pride that lives in each one of us. When it's focused inward, it enslaves us to perceptions and pursuits of success, beauty, competency, security, and a coveted reputation, and in the process heaps upon us burdens we can't bear. When we fail, it pressures us to lie and deceive in order to hide what we feel too ashamed (too proud) to admit. When focused outward, it heaps great burdens upon ("lords it over") others. That's why God mercifully opposes our pride (1 Peter 5:5).

Jesus' call to servanthood is a paradoxical call to freedom. It's freedom from the oppressive pressure of trying to meet an imaginary, vague, and therefore illusive standard of being "good enough," and the chronic shame of never meeting that standard. And when Jesus sets us free from this, we lose the shame of not being "great" and can see ourselves more as we truly are: very needy people who desperately need the Son of Man to serve us in every conceivable way. It also results in our freeing others from the tyranny of being used by us to serve our vain pursuit of an impossible self-image and frees us to see them for who they really are and what they really need, and really love them through doing what we can to meet their real needs.

In God's eyes, this is true greatness. And it's true greatness in most people's eyes as well, because most people admire those who sacrificially love others more than high achievers who have used or neglected others to reach their achievements.

Through his startling imagery, Jesus faithfully shows us the path to true freedom: the loving humility to allow God to be who he truly is and serve us, and the loving humility to allow others to be who they truly are and to serve them. And any church that becomes a loving society of members who "in humility count others more significant than [themselves]" (Phil. 2:3) will discover great treasure in the truth that "God . . . gives grace to the humble" (1 Peter 5:5).

PRAYER

Father, thank you for your faithful Son who revealed this counterintuitive but experientially confirmed truth that true greatness is seen in the loving humility of those who, like your Son, seek less to be served but to serve. Whatever it takes, help me become truly great. In Jesus' name, amen.

MEDITATE MORE

Read Philippians 2:1–11.

74

And he took bread, and when he had given thanks, he broke it and gave it to them, saying, "This is my body, which is given for you. Do this in remembrance of me." LUKE 22:19

Jesus Shows You How a Heavy Heart Gives Thanks

GOD IS FAITHFUL . . . TO COMMAND YOU TO GIVE THANKS IN TERRIBLE CIRCUMSTANCES

No one in the history of the world was burdened in his soul like Jesus as he shared with the disciples that last meal before his execution. He fully knew the price he was about to pay to take away the sins of the world (John 1:29), that in hours he would be "crushed for our iniquities" (Isa. 53:5). What grief and sorrow he bore.

And yet, as Jesus held the bread in his hands, before the poignant moment he broke it, he *gave thanks*. With an incomparably heavy heart, Jesus *gave thanks*. With the horror of anticipated horror pressing in on his consciousness, Jesus *gave thanks*. As he was walking into the deepest valley of the shadow of death ever experienced by a human, Jesus *gave thanks*. And then, understanding its full meaning, he broke the bread.

When the Spirit of Jesus tells us not to let our hearts be troubled (John 14:1), and to give thanks in all circumstances (1 Thess. 5:18), we can know that we have a high priest who is able to sympathize with us in our heavy-hearted suffering (Heb. 4:15). And he left us an example, that we "might follow in his steps" (1 Peter 2:21).

The author of Hebrews shows us this example when he tells us to look "to Jesus, the founder and perfecter of our faith, who for the joy that was set before him endured the cross, despising the shame" (Heb. 12:2). In the face of unquantifiable, inexpressible evil, Jesus believed the Father's promises that his sacrificial death would overcome the worst, hellish evil in the world (John 3:16–17), that "out of the anguish of his soul" he would "see his offspring" and "prolong his days" (Isa. 53:10–11), and that if he humbled himself under God's mighty hand, his Father would exalt him at the proper time (1 Peter 5:6), and every knee would bow and tongue confess that he was Lord to the glory of his Father (Phil. 2:11). It was believing the Father's promised future grace of joy that enabled Jesus to give thanks in his unfathomably terrible circumstances.

And Jesus' faithful example shows us how we can give thanks in our agonizing circumstances. Because Jesus has "overcome the world" for us (John 16:33), we are able to "believe in God [and] also in [him]" (John 14:1) that God knows "the end from the beginning" (Isa. 46:10), is working all things together for our good (Rom. 8:28), will complete the good work he began in us despite how things look now (Phil. 1:6), will make us more than conquerors through Christ (Rom. 8:37–39), will remember every troubled tear our suffering provokes (Ps. 56:8), and someday will himself wipe them away forever (Rev. 21:4).

Giving thanks when our hearts are heavy is not only possible, but God's command that we do so is an expression of his faithfulness. Because the act of giving thanks is what forces us to remember the joy set before us in God's promises of future grace, which is the grace of joy we need to endure the suffering before us today.

PRAYER

Father, thank you for what sorrow and horror Jesus endured on my behalf, and for his remarkable example of giving thanks to you in the moment of his unspeakable grief and fear. And thank you for faithfully commanding me to give thanks in my suffering so that I remember the promised joys you have set before me. In Jesus' name, amen.

MEDITATE MORE

Read Luke 22:14–20. Do you see how Jesus' gratitude to his Father was sustaining him at that moment?

What God Does When You Don't Insist on Your Own Way

GOD IS FAITHFUL . . . WHEN HE CALLS YOU TO DIE TO YOUR SELFISH PREFERENCES

What was Paul talking about here? He wasn't delivering a universal ethic. He wasn't implying that God, being love (1 John 4:8), doesn't have the right to insist on his own way, or that there aren't situations in which the most loving thing is to insist on our own way. He was addressing the sinful proclivity you and I have to count ourselves more significant than others and our default tendency to look to our own interests rather than the interests of others (Phil. 2:3–4). Paul was saying that *love does not selfishly insist on its own way.*

And in saying this, Paul was putting his finger on something we struggle with every day. We find not insisting on our own way difficult for the same reason we find being patient and kind, not envying or boasting, not being arrogant or rude, and not being irritable or resentful difficult (1 Cor. 13:4–7): love requires dying to our selfish preferences.

Having personal preferences is not wrong. God created us to prefer certain things and not prefer certain things. The diversity of personalities, abilities, interests, insights, aesthetic tastes, culinary enjoyments, convictions, priorities, and so on benefits us all immensely in countless ways and adds to the richness of the human experience. The world would be a boring place if everyone shared our own preferences (not to mention we'd probably not survive long).

But one of the ways our different preferences are meant to enrich us the most is that they provide endless ways to express love to one another. One of the most practical, tangible ways others experience our love for them is when we seek to honor their interests, not just our own, and humbly count them more significant than ourselves.

Think of a memorable time when someone lovingly (not manipulatively) did that for you. How did that make you feel? I doubt very much you felt good about getting the better of them and winning the preference contest. You likely felt both honored and humbled. And it likely increased your trust in that person because you can trust someone who you know honors and looks out for your interests. And it likely drew out a desire to be generous, magnanimous, and someone they could trust as well. That's the relational and spiritual health love produces.

Imagine the relational and spiritual health of a church filled by Christians who do not selfishly insist on their own way because they are following their faithful Savior who "did not count equality with God a thing to be grasped, but emptied himself, by taking the form of a servant . . . [and] humbled himself by becoming obedient to the point of death, even death on a cross" (Phil. 2:6–8). Imagine the collective generosity and mutual trust it would foster and the rancorous conflicts it would be spared. Imagine the refuge and restoration a church like this would provide people and marriages and families damaged by the evil effects of those who'd subjected them to their own evil ways.

This is the sweet fruit of the love command to not insist on our own way. And God is faithful to produce it and spread it if we are faithful to obey it.

PRAYER

Father, forgive me for every time I've insisted on my own way and give me grace today to die to my selfish preferences, that I and those around me might experience the rich relational and spiritual health of the love of Christ, in whose name I pray, amen.

MEDITATE MORE

Review 1 Corinthians 13 to encourage your desire to live a life of Christlike love.

When Jesus Doesn't Meet Your Expectations

GOD IS FAITHFUL . . . TO MEET YOUR GREATEST NEEDS, NOT YOUR EXPECTATIONS

This verse above was Nathanael's response to his friend Philip, who'd just announced he'd found the Messiah: Jesus of Nazareth. Nathanael didn't expect the Messiah to come from Nazareth. And he was just one in a long line of persons whose expectations Jesus didn't meet.

The people of Israel expected the Son of David to be born in the city of David (Mic. 5:2), but not by the coincidence of a census, and certainly not in such ignobility (Luke 2:7). They expected him to be hailed upon his arrival, but not by shepherds and pagan magi, and certainly not ignored by Israel's religious leaders, who knew all the prophecies by heart.

They didn't expect him to grow up in Galilee (John 7:52), let alone Nazareth, the son of an unconnected, uneducated tradesman. They didn't expect him to appear as an itinerant rabbi with a school of disciples that consisted of fishermen, tax collectors, and zealots. They didn't expect him to confront pious Jews more than the Roman occupiers, and they certainly didn't expect him to find more faith in a Roman centurion than in all the people of Israel (Luke 7:9).

The Samaritan woman in John 4 never expected him to appear at her well, the paralytic in John 5 never expected him to appear at his pool, and the man born blind never expected him to appear in his sight (John 9). The widow of Nain in Luke 7 never expected him to show up at her son's funeral and raise him, and Mary and Martha never expected him *not* to show up and heal Lazarus (John 11).

No one expected the Messiah, the Son of David, to be convicted of blasphemy by the Sanhedrin and be brutally executed without dignity by the

Romans outside the other city of David. And no one expected him to actually rise from the dead three days later.

Jesus came into the world at a desperate time in a desperate way. It wasn't the way people expected him to come. It wasn't for the reasons they expected him to come. He did not come to meet their expectations but to love them in the ways they most desperately needed—a love exceeding all our expectations.

All these things had been prophesied; Jesus had been long expected. But when they actually encountered the Messiah, it was in unexpected ways at unexpected times in unexpected places.

And that's generally how Jesus works with us too. He didn't come to meet our expectations; he came to meet our deepest, most desperate needs. So, he typically shows up in unexpected ways, at unexpected times, in unexpected places.

So, look for him in the unexpected place. And it may be in the most desperate place, yours or another's. But know this: he will meet you in the place that will, if you trust him, cause his good news to eventually bring you the greatest joy (Luke 2:10)—the place you are most likely to really adore him.

PRAYER

Father, the ways Jesus didn't meet expectations reminds me how much more I must trust your promises than my perceptions. I welcome your Son's presence any place he wishes to meet me, especially the places where I will most experience your great love. In Jesus' name, amen.

MEDITATE MORE

Read John 3:1–21 and observe Jesus not meeting Nicodemus's expectations.

Why Your Spiritual Growth Can Seem Slow

GOD IS FAITHFUL . . . TO PATIENTLY TRANSFORM YOU INTO THE IMAGE OF HIS SON

We live in an age that highly values speed and efficiency. We're always striving for faster transportation, faster computers, faster internet access, faster ways to absorb information, faster means of production, faster delivery systems—everything should be faster. As Christians living in an age of speed, we shouldn't be surprised to find ourselves assuming that we should be able to find ways to speed up our spiritual growth.

But this isn't a biblical assumption. When we look at Scripture, creation, redemptive history, and our own experiences, we see a God who is not in a hurry. We see a God whose patience almost exasperates us at times. And if we look carefully, we see that the most important things take a long time to grow and mature. They can't be rushed.

Our culture places a high value on knowledge accumulation. That's why our educational systems are designed more to fill heads with information than character transformation. Even Christian educational systems tend to be designed that way.

But Christians are disciples of Jesus. And as Eugene Peterson said, "A disciple is a learner, but not in the academic setting of a schoolroom, rather at the work site of a craftsman."[32] A disciple is an apprentice of Jesus, who walks with him long enough to learn to be like him in all respects. God set up the Christian life so that we really come to know Christ, not merely that we become knowledgeable about Christian theology.

Really knowing someone requires a certain comprehensive and nuanced understanding of them. And there's no way to really know someone without spending a lot of time with them, conversing much with them, observing them, and truly loving them—everything it takes to have a mutual level of trust with them so that they are willing to disclose themselves to us. Such a relationship isn't developed easily or quickly with another physical human being. To really get to know Christ requires an additional level of spiritual discernment. These things can't be merely learned in a classroom or sanctuary. It takes a long time and it isn't acquired through what we typically understand efficient to mean.

That's why God has designed the Christian life the way he has. All its dimensions—like Scripture meditation, corporate and private prayer, corporate and private worship, small-group participation, and the countless inefficient, time-consuming ways we're called to serve others—are designed so that over time we become transformed into the image of his Son (Rom. 8:29). And there are no life hacks for holiness.

Our spiritual growth might seem slow to us, but God isn't slow; he's patient (2 Peter 3:9). That's why the fruit of the Spirit includes patience. We need patience as God faithfully apprentices us to Christ so that we patiently, carefully, rigorously learn our craft, the holy craft of divine love, from the Master. God is not in a hurry, so we don't have to be either.

PRAYER

Father, forgive me for every time my wrong assumptions have fueled my sinful impatience over my spiritual growth. I don't want to merely know about your Son, I want to really know him. So do today's work, however inefficient it may appear to me, to transform me into the image of Christ, in whose name I pray, amen.

MEDITATE MORE

Review John 15:1–8 and consider the slow, organic metaphor Jesus uses to describe the Christian life.

The Benefits of Your Slow Growth

WHY GOD IS FAITHFUL ... TO TRANSFORM YOU SLOWLY

Paul's original readers would have had a deeper experiential understanding of his metaphor than many of us do. For most of human history, most people's lives aligned with the relatively slow cyclical rhythms of the seasons. Life was demanding and difficult because it had a primary, and at times ruthless, focus on subsistence, and so was largely dictated by the annual migration patterns of fish and herd animals, plant and fruit cultivation and harvesting, rainy seasons, and available sunlight.

One of the things this did was produce and reinforce in the minds of people, because of sheer necessity, an understanding of the value of slow, incremental progress toward an aimed-for reward.

But we live in a different world. Due to the rapid evolution of technologies and industrial processes over the past two hundred years, most of our lives aren't shaped by slow seasonal rhythms but by the fast forces of the competitive global market. And this has, in some ways, distorted our perspective on time and led us to undervalue the benefits of slow growth.

But God created us as organisms, not machines. That's why Jesus frequently used agricultural metaphors to illustrate spiritual realities, drawing from sowers (Matt. 13:1–9), reapers (John 4:35–38), wheat fields (Matt. 13:24–30), mustard seeds (Matt. 13:31–32), fruit-bearing trees (Matt. 7:16–18), and vines (John 15:1–8). And so did his apostles, like Paul. And like Paul's readers, Jesus' original hearers would have intuitively understood the gradual, progressive nature of the realities he was referring to in ways many of us might miss.

Disciples are slow grown, and fruit bearing typically comes after an arduous time of maturation. The same is true for churches, which is why we rightly call the process of starting new churches "church planting" and not "church manufacturing."

As organisms, God designed us to cultivate, not manufacture, habits of obedience and holiness incrementally, because the gradual nature of the process trains us to live by faith rather than by our momentary perceptions and emotions. The endurance gained through waiting teaches us to trust more in the truth of what God says than the urgent impulses caused by what we currently see or feel. That's why David instructs us to "live in the land and cultivate faithfulness" (Ps. 37:3 NASB). We learn how to be faithful through the rigors of having to work at it.

The long-term beneficial effect of slow, incremental transformation through the exercise of habit over time results in deeper, richer, more complex and nuanced affections for God, and integrates our beliefs into our whole being.

God's ways with us are perfectly faithful (Deut. 32:4). To us they might seem needlessly slow and inefficient. But none of God's ways are needless, and God is not slow; he's patient (2 Peter 3:9). As it applies to our spiritual maturity, he calls us to plant and water, cultivate and weed, and wait for all the elements and factors outside our control, but not outside his, to play their necessary parts. And in his good time, he gives us our growth.

PRAYER

Father, thank you for the patient, deliberate, incremental approach to my spiritual growth. Teach me greater patience with and deeper appreciation for your ways, and to remain faithful in my cultivating responsibilities as you give me the growth I need. In Jesus' name, amen.

MEDITATE MORE

Read Luke 13:6–9. What was Jesus getting at in highlighting the vinedresser's patience?

79

Therefore, preparing your minds for action, and being sober-minded, set your hope fully on the grace that will be brought to you at the revelation of Jesus Christ. 1 PETER 1:13

What's Your Mindset?

GOD IS FAITHFUL . . . TO HELP YOU PREPARE YOUR MIND FOR ACTION

Our mindsets massively influence how we perceive our circumstances. What we expect shapes how we respond. If we expect peace, we will resent having to fight. If we expect rest, we will resent having to endure. If we expect leisure, we will resent having to work hard.

This is why it's so important for us to "prepare our minds for action." It's clear in the New Testament that the Holy Spirit wants us to prepare to fight a grueling war, to run an endurance race, and to engage in the difficult work of kingdom farming. Paul captures all three analogies in his exhortation to Timothy:

> Share in suffering as a good soldier of Christ Jesus. No soldier gets entangled in civilian pursuits, since his aim is to please the one who enlisted him. An athlete is not crowned unless he competes according to the rules. It is the hard-working farmer who ought to have the first share of the crops. Think over what I say, for the Lord will give you understanding in everything. (2 Tim. 2:3–7)

Paul wants Timothy and us to "think over" what he says. He wants us to engage in expectation-shaping thinking because Paul knows the crucial importance of mindsets. He tells us to "set your minds on things that are above, not on things that are on earth" (Col. 3:2), since "those who live according to the flesh set their minds on the things of the flesh, but those who live according to the Spirit set their minds on the things of the Spirit" (Rom. 8:5).

So, the Holy Spirit speaking in 2 Timothy 2:3–7 wants us to have a soldier's mindset, which is very different from a civilian's. A soldier expects to suffer the rigors and dangers of war; a civilian does not.

The Spirit wants us to have the mindset of an athlete, which is very different from that of a spectator. "Every athlete [expects to exercise] self-control in all things" in order to win the prize; a spectator does not (1 Cor. 9:25).

And the Spirit wants us to have a farmer's mindset, which is very different from an average customer's. A farmer expects to work hard for long hours, over long months, in all kinds of weather, to realize a harvest; a customer does not.

Civilians are passive during war; spectators are passive during competition; an average customer is passive during the growing season. As Christians, we are not called to leisurely passivity, but to rigorous activity.

Therefore, we must prepare our minds for action. Sometimes this preparation is preventative (to preempt discouragement), and sometimes it's restorative (to revive courage). The former is always helpful, but all of us repeatedly require the latter. We lose perspective and forget that in this age, war, not peace, is the norm; vigilant self-control, not indulgent rest, is the norm; difficult cultivation, not easy picking, is the norm.

So, what's your mindset? A soldier's or civilian's? An athlete's or spectator's? A hardworking farmer's or a customer's? Think it over. For if you do, "the Lord will give you understanding in everything" (2 Tim. 2:7).

PRAYER

Father, thank you for your Spirit's faithful exhortation to me to prepare my mind for action and not passivity. Help me today to actively engage in fighting, training, and cultivating whenever it's called for, and see it as my privileged calling, and not an imposition on my entitled leisure. In Jesus' name, amen.

MEDITATE MORE

Read 2 Timothy 2:1–13 to see how Paul seeks to help Timothy prepare his mind for action.

80

Give thanks in all circumstances; for this is the will of God in Christ Jesus for you. 1 THESSALONIANS 5:18

Why God Commands You to Give Thanks

GOD IS FAITHFUL . . . TO HELP YOU SEE MORE GRACE BY GIVING MORE THANKS

The spiritual cost to us of being ungrateful is much higher than we might think. Thanklessness is not merely the absence of verbalizing a "thank you." It is a symptom of spiritual sickness, of spiritual poverty, because it is taking for granted and not appreciating grace being shown to us.

Parents know what this looks like. Children, being born self-centered sinners, naturally take for granted all the blood, sweat, tears, and dollars their parents invest in them. So, parents are frequently reminding their children to give thanks. "Remember to thank your mother for making dinner." "Thank your grandma for that nice birthday gift." "Have you finished your graduation thank-you cards yet?"

Why do parents do this? It's not because they enjoy watching their children jump through social courtesy hoops. They want their children to learn to see the grace they've received, feel the joy of gratitude, and appropriately honor the grace giver. They instinctively know that these things are a sign of a spiritually and relationally healthy person. And they instinctively know ingratitude indicates a level of self-centeredness which, if left untreated, will become spiritually and relationally harmful and impoverishing.

In such parents we see a reflection of God's heart for us. When God commands us to thank him, it's not because he gets a kick out of hearing "thank you." It's because he wants us to be spiritually healthy and prosperous. He wants us to experience the joy of recognizing when we've received a gracious gift from him, and he knows that our expressing grateful joy through verbalizing our gratitude—whether out loud, silently, or in writing—completes our experience of joy. And he knows that thanklessness is a dangerous symptom of the spiritual disease of unbelief (Rom. 1:21).

And that's why God so often commands and exhorts us through the biblical writers to give thanks to him. These kinds of statements are sprinkled throughout the Psalms:

> I will give thanks to the LORD.—Psalm 9:1; and many more
> Give thanks to the LORD.—Psalm 105:1; and many more
> Enter his gates with thanksgiving.—Psalm 100:4
> Surely the righteous shall give thanks to your name.—Psalm 140:13

And Paul weaves references of thanks to God all through his letters:

> I give thanks to my God always for you.—1 Corinthians 1:4
> I do not cease to give thanks for you.—Ephesians 1:16
> I thank my God in all my remembrance of you.—Philippians 1:3
> We ought always to give thanks to God.—2 Thessalonians 1:3
> Give thanks in all circumstances.—1 Thessalonians 5:18

These are not the commands of a vain deity. They are the merciful prescription of the Great Physician; they are the faithful reminders of our loving Father. God intends his frequent reminders to help us increasingly see how much grace we continually receive from him and increasingly experience the profoundly healthy and deep joy of feeling grateful. The more we see, savor, and express gratitude to God, the more glory he receives as the grace-Giver, and we get the joy of being grace-receivers and gratitude-feelers.

PRAYER

Father, I am happily redundant when I say thank you for commanding me to thank you! Not only is it right for me to thank you but knowing that obeying these commands leads to my seeing and savoring more of your grace turns these commands into graces! Thank you for grace upon grace! In Jesus' gracious name, amen.

MEDITATE MORE

Look up each Scripture reference above to take advantage of the grace they provide you to give thanks to the Lord.

81

Oh, the depth of the riches and wisdom and knowledge of God! How unsearchable are his judgments and how inscrutable his ways! ROMANS 11:33

God Is Faithful in What He Doesn't Say

GOD IS FAITHFUL . . . IN THE "DARK MATTER" OF DIVINE REVELATION

We know that God is very wise in the knowledge he reveals, even if some aspects are difficult to understand (2 Peter 3:16). But God is just as wise in what he doesn't say, even though this causes us different difficulties, leading us to ask, "Why, O LORD?" (Ps. 10:1).

We might call the wise silence of God the "dark matter" of divine revelation. There is real substance in what we can't see, but it's detected with a different kind of inquiry. Let's briefly explore the wisdom of God's silence by looking at two controversial examples that bookend the story of Scripture: the creation account and the second coming.

The thirty-one simple, Spirit-inspired verses that contain the Genesis 1 creation story tell us God created the world in a certain sequence, but they gloss over an astronomical amount of detail. Why didn't God say more?

Here's one reason we can deduce: God chose a creation account that would provide an essential understanding of cosmic and human origins for his people over the span of multiple millennia, in countless different cultures with many different worldviews, conceptions of time, levels of education, and stages of technological advancement. It had to be comprehensible to pre-scientific, primitive, and illiterate peoples, and able to withstand withering critique by the most brilliant, educated minds of antiquity, as well as in the modern scientific age. It had to be simple enough for a child to understand and complex enough to account for a paleontologist's discoveries. And that's what we have. Genesis 1 reminds us that "the foolishness of God is wiser than men" (1 Cor. 1:25).

The first coming of the Messiah was prophesied, yet his people were caught off guard when he appeared because he fulfilled the prophecies in ways they didn't expect. Similarly, we have prophecies concerning Jesus' return, but the meaning of the symbolic presentation of its timing and surrounding events in Scripture have provoked much debate throughout church history. Why didn't God say more?

Here's one reason we can deduce: God intends "the Son of Man [to come] at an hour [we] do not expect" (Luke 12:40) so that his followers will "stay awake at all times" (Luke 21:36), and keep our lamps trimmed (Matt. 25:1–13). God knows our fight against indwelling sin, and our sense of urgency for the mission is better served by knowing Christ's return could be at any time than that he will be long delayed (Matt. 24:45–51; 1 Cor. 7:29).

These two very brief examples serve as reminders that God is wise and intentional in what he does and doesn't make clear to us. Some of his purposes regarding things he doesn't explicitly say we can deduce over time or from other things he says. But some things will remain "unsearchable" and "inscrutable" to us. And living by faith in him requires that we increasingly trust him regarding what he conceals as we do regarding what he reveals. "For the word of the LORD is upright, and all his work is done in faithfulness" (Ps. 33:4).

PRAYER

Father, with Paul I say, "Oh, the depth of [your] riches and wisdom and knowledge!" Thank you for all that you faithfully reveal to me and for all you faithfully conceal from me. Whenever I'm troubled by something you choose to conceal, give me the grace to "not occupy myself with things too great and too marvelous for me" (Ps. 131:1). In Jesus' name, amen.

MEDITATE MORE

Reflect on Psalm 131, where David teaches us one faithful way to respond to God's inscrutable ways.

82

For freedom Christ has set us free; stand firm therefore, and do not submit again to a yoke of slavery. GALATIANS 5:1

Always "Be" First

GOD IS FAITHFUL . . . TO LIBERATE US FROM SATAN'S IDENTITY ENSLAVEMENT

How many of your familiar, recurring anxieties and fears are rooted in the belief that if you don't do ____, you'll never have ____, and therefore never become ____? How much does this belief influence how you invest your time, energy, and money? How much does it fuel your social media activity, battles with envy, relational conflicts, perhaps even your ministry labors?

The *Do. Have. Be.* virus has been around a long time. It infected us in Eden (Gen. 3:4–5) when the serpent successfully hacked our operating systems with this promise: if you eat the fruit (do), you will acquire God's wisdom (have), and become like God (be). But this turned out to be a diabolically false gospel. The virus corrupted our operating systems, leading us to pursue our identity in a way that never works. This has been the history of fallen humanity ever since: a destructive, despairing rat race to hell.

Jesus came to deliver us from this hellish rat race by declaring to us the true gospel that if we're born again, we have a new nature with an operating system that restores our identity code from the corrupt *Do. Have. Be.* virus back to the Manufacturer's original: *Be. Do. Have.*

This is one of the great truths of the gospel through which God intends for us to experience "the freedom of the glory of the children of God" (Rom. 8:21): We are ____, therefore we do ____, resulting in our having ____. *Be. Do. Have.* Living out of the "be" instead of the "do" makes all the difference in the world. Instead of chasing our identity by trying so hard to "do," we receive our true identity (be) as a free gift of grace from our loving Creator God (Eph. 1:4–5; 2:8). We are free to follow our Good Shepherd along the righteous paths of good works (do) he prepared for us (Eph. 2:10). And we trust him to supply (have) everything we need (Phil. 4:19), knowing we will never again want for any good, necessary thing.

Is it any wonder Satan works so hard to get us to live according to his old corrupt code? If he can deceive us into believing the *Do. Have. Be.* lie, we "submit again to [his] yoke of slavery" (Gal. 5:1). He can keep us too occupied chasing an elusive identity to be any serious threat to his influence in the world. If he can get entire churches and Christian subcultures to live by this lie, he significantly slows the spread of Jesus' kingdom.

"For freedom Christ has [faithfully done everything necessary to] set us free," so we must "stand firm" against Satan's schemes to enslave us again under the old "yoke" of the *Do. Have. Be.* ethic (Gal. 5:1). The new birth Jesus purchased for us and has freely given us liberates us to take his easy yoke of God's *Be. Do. Have.* ethic.

When it comes to understanding the role our identity plays in our experiencing the greatest joy and deepest contentment available to us, we must remember that God is faithful to instruct us to always "be" first.

PRAYER

Father, thank you for faithfully doing everything necessary through your Son to set me free from the satanic yoke of trying to achieve an identity through what I accomplish and acquire. And thank you for graciously gifting me an identity in you that fuels my faith to do the good works you've prepared for me and have all my needs supplied you. In Jesus' name, amen.

MEDITATE MORE

Read Ephesians 1:3–14 and pray for the strength to comprehend the glorious identity God has given you.

83

"And you will know the truth, and the truth will set you free."

JOHN 8:32

What Our Insecurity Tells Us

GOD IS FAITHFUL . . . TO MAKE YOUR INSECURITIES
A GREAT MERCY TO YOU

When people are insecure, they can express it in very different ways, depending on their temperament as well as values and conditioned habits shaped by their past experiences. In one person, insecurity might look like meekness, compliance, and always assuming blame. In another, it might look like bravado, defiance, and never admitting wrong. Insecurity moves one person to avoid attention if possible while it moves another to demand as much attention as possible.

Despite its different manifestations, we're all familiar with the experience of feeling insecure. But what is this feeling telling us?

Insecurity is an internal fear alarm instructing us to take some protective action because we feel vulnerable to some kind of danger. But in our culture, "insecure" most commonly refers to a person feeling a significant lack of self-confidence, or a powerful fear of others' disapproval or rejection, or a chronic sense of inferiority. If we feel insecure, our internal alarm is instructing us to take some action to protect our identity, which we fear is being threatened.

Our identity is who we understand ourselves to be at the core, our essential self. Or it's what we want to believe (and want others to believe) is our essential self, even if it's not who we really are.

Where do we derive our sense of identity from? Our identity is tied to what we believe is most important, what we really want, what we really believe offers us hope, what we orient our life around, what we most love. In other words, we derive our identity from our god, the person or thing we believe has the greatest power to determine our purpose, value, and happiness. Our god is what we can't help but pursue, because we believe our god's promises will bring us the greatest happiness.

As Christians, when our sense of identity feels threatened, our insecurity is telling us something very important, which is a great mercy, though it almost never feels like a mercy because it feels like fear, inadequacy, failure, or condemnation. It makes us feel vulnerable and uncertain.

So, rather than examine or admit the cause of our insecurity, we might try to compensate in those ways shaped by our temperament, values, and conditioned habits. Or we might try to escape through things—sometimes harmful, even addictive things—that dull or distract or fantasize away our identity-fear, at least temporarily. These are all faithless ways of attempting to reduce our identity fears, and since "whatever does not proceed from faith is sin" (Rom. 14:23), they are sinful. And they're futile, because they only medicate the symptoms of our insecurity, but don't address the cause.

And in not addressing the cause, we withhold from ourselves the mercy God offers those who bring their insecurity to him. For God faithfully designed insecurity as a warning indicator that something's wrong with what we understand God, or some other god, is telling us about who we are. He means for us to examine it in order that we might escape danger. That's why it's a mercy. In the next chapter we'll see how God, as our faithful Father, uses insecurity as an invitation to us to receive the truth about who we really are in Christ. And when you "know the truth . . . the truth will set you free."

PRAYER

Father, "I praise you, for I am fearfully and wonderfully made" (Ps. 139:14). You have even made my identity-fears a means of grace that I might escape deception and experience "the freedom of the glory of the children of God" (Rom. 8:21). Help me respond faithfully and allow you to expose any false things I have believed so that I will fully know the truth that sets me free. In Jesus' name, amen.

MEDITATE MORE

Review Romans 8:31–39 and remember that if God is for you, nothing can stand against you (v. 31).

84

*But to all who did receive him, who believed in his name, he gave
the right to become children of God.* JOHN 1:12

God's Marvelous Invitation
Hidden in Your Insecurity

GOD IS FAITHFUL . . . TO REVEAL YOUR
MULTIDIMENSIONAL IDENTITY

Through our faith in Jesus, we have become children of God! That is now
our true identity as Christians. More personally, through *your* belief in
Jesus, this is *your* identity: a child of God. And really knowing this truth will
set you free from the spiritual disorder of insecurity.

But this is not your sole identity as a Christian. God has given you another dimension of your identity in Christ that plays an important role in
addressing your insecurity.

One of the marvelous gifts of your new birth and mine is that "we,
though many, are one body in Christ, and individually members one of another" (Rom. 12:5). What this means is that when, through Christ, God
makes us his children, he gives us a multidimensional identity: a collective
dimension as a member united to Christ's whole body, and an individual
dimension as an "indispensable" member (1 Cor. 12:22). As Christians,
both dimensions become part of our core being, our essential selves. For
there are ways we can only know God and know ourselves in the context
of the collective body, and ways we can only know God and ourselves as
individual members.

It's important to have this framework in view as we continue from the
previous chapter to understand how God has faithfully provided a way to set
us free from our insecurities. We've already reflected on the mercy of God's
design in making our identity insecurities a kind of warning indicator to let
us know something's wrong with what we believe about who we are at the
core of our being.

But as Christians, our insecurity is more than a warning; it's also an invitation. God is inviting us to address our false beliefs so that we will "know the truth, and the truth will set [us] free" (John 8:32). He wants us to know who we really are in Christ so that we will experience "the freedom of the glory of the children of God" (Rom. 8:21).

But because God has given us a multidimensional identity, his invitation to bring our insecurities to him to examine what functional beliefs are giving rise to them is twofold: he wants us to come to him privately as individual members to humbly confess our sins and fears and bring Scripture to bear on our false beliefs. And he wants us to come to him in the presence of other trusted members of the body to humbly confess and receive the body's help in overcoming our false beliefs. Because just as there are unique ways God reveals himself and who we are as individuals and unique ways he does this in the context of the body, there are unique graces we receive from the Holy Spirit as individuals and unique graces we receive in the context of the body. Both are uniquely important ways we come to the throne of grace to help us in time of need (Heb. 4:16).

This is the remarkable invitation God extends to us through our insecurities, as well as through most other needs we have: to learn what it means to be a child of God. And in accepting his invitation and pursuing his grace in both dimensions, we will come to know the truth that sets us free.

PRAYER

Father, I stand in awe of the gift you've given me in giving me the right, through your Son, to become your child. There is far more to my identity than I have yet understood. By your grace, I receive your twofold invitation to grow in my understanding as an individual member and in the context of your church. In Jesus' name, amen.

MEDITATE MORE

Read Ephesians 4:1–16 where Paul beautifully describes the multidimensional nature of the children of God who comprise the church.

85

"You therefore must be perfect, as your heavenly Father is perfect."
MATTHEW 5:48

How God Frees You from Perfectionism

GOD IS FAITHFUL . . . TO PROVIDE YOU THE PERFECTION YOU CANNOT PERFORM

"The perfect is the enemy of the good," says an old adage. Productivity experts have put a twist on it to emphasize the consequence: "The perfect is the enemy of the done." Both sayings are true. At times, we've all neglected to do what we can for fear of not doing it perfectly. Our term for this is "perfectionism."

Perfectionism is not the same as the pursuit of excellence. Pursuing excellence is doing something as well as possible within a given set of talent, resource, and time limits. But perfectionism is a compulsion to do something as well as possible, period—to the neglect of other necessary things. And what's usually fueling it is an exaggerated desire for acceptance or fear of rejection. And the wonderful news is that God wants us to live free of its tyrannical grip on us.

But given that quote from Jesus above, we might wonder if this is true. "You must be perfect" doesn't sound like freedom from perfectionism.

Jesus gives us a clue in another statement he made shortly before this one: "Do not think that I have come to abolish the Law or the Prophets; I have not come to abolish them but to fulfill them" (Matt. 5:17). Jesus came to meet God's demand for perfection for us. That's why the New Testament authors write of him things like, "By a single offering he has perfected for all time those who are being sanctified" (Heb. 10:14).

So, God *does* demand our perfection and then graciously and freely provides us, through Christ's redemptive work, the perfection we cannot perform. He gives us Christ's imputed perfection now (2 Cor. 5:21) and promises us sinless perfection in the age to come (Rev. 21:3–4). This is what frees us to live, not under the heavy perfectionistic yoke of the law, but under Christ's easy yoke of grace (Rom. 6:14).

What makes this wonderfully practical news for us is that God wants us to experience the refreshment of getting our eyes off our imperfect, inadequate, insufficient selves and onto our all-sufficient Savior (Heb. 12:2). He wants to free us from the enslaving "approval of man" (Gal. 1:10) and the snare of the "fear of man" (Prov. 29:25) that fuels much of our perfectionism so we can pursue the higher, greater call of love (1 Cor. 14:1; 1 Tim. 1:5).

God has been faithful to provide you, through your faith in Christ, all the perfection you need to please him. And if perfectionism has an inordinate influence on you, God will faithfully design circumstances to defeat your best efforts to earn the approval you seek or avoid the rejection you fear so that you will learn where your perfection and freedom really come from.

In Christ, you are free! You are free to follow Jesus imperfectly. And you are free to pursue excellence, provided that it doesn't turn into a false idol of perfectionism. Because God wants you to remain free to not neglect living by childlike, dependent faith in Christ through authentic acts of love (Gal. 5:6).

PRAYER

Father, thank you for so mercifully and faithfully providing me the perfection you demand but I am unable to perform and giving me Jesus' easy yoke of grace. Free me from any perfectionism that remains in me, so I am free to love others as you have loved me. In Jesus' name, amen.

MEDITATE MORE

Read Galatians 5 to review how to walk by the Spirit so you won't give yourself to gratifying the enslaving desires of the flesh (v. 16).

86

Whatever is true, whatever is honorable, whatever is just, whatever is pure, whatever is lovely, whatever is commendable, if there is any excellence, if there is anything worthy of praise, think about these things. PHILIPPIANS 4:8

Think about These Things

GOD IS FAITHFUL . . . TO PROVIDE YOU AN ESCAPE FROM A SINFUL TRAIN OF THOUGHT

Where do your thoughts come from? They're coming from somewhere. But much of the time it's probably not at all obvious to you where they're coming from.

If we want to know where our thoughts are coming from, the first thing is to look at our emotional frame of mind. What specifically is the governing emotion shaping our mindset—fear, anxiety, anger, disappointment, discouragement, grief, sadness, hope, excitement, pride, joy, desire, anticipation? The reason we look here is because whatever is fueling this governing emotion is what's feeding our thoughts.

And what fuels our governing emotion is some functional belief. An ungodly functional belief about something important to us gives rise to an ungodly governing emotion, which frames our ungodly pattern of thinking and feeds our specific ungodly thoughts.

So, what do we do when we're stuck in a sinful train of thought? The Holy Spirit speaking through the apostle Paul faithfully shows us in the text above: we "think about these things."

But you and I both know we can't by sheer willpower just stop thinking unrighteous thoughts and start thinking righteous thoughts. But that's not what Paul (or the Holy Spirit) means. We know this by looking at the list of things Paul tells us to think about. Note how abstract the concepts are that Paul lists. The last time you struggled to escape a compulsive train of negative thought, how much help were concepts like truth, honor, justice, purity, or excellence? To the degree they remained abstract, probably no help at all.

Paul never intended these concepts to remain abstract. That's why he wrote "whatever is" before each one. Paul knew that giving rise to our negative, sinful thoughts are specific false, dishonorable, unjust, impure, ugly, disgraceful, and detestable functional beliefs. "Whatever" these functional sinful beliefs (or unbeliefs) are must be confronted and replaced with "whatever is" the appropriate, God-dependent belief. When we address our functional belief problem, we address our governing emotion problem, and ultimately, we address our thought problem.

When we're struggling with distracting, demanding sinful thoughts, God wants us to know that we're not mere victims who must simply endure a miserable ride, trapped in a negative train of thoughts. He wants us to seize the controls he's provided us, switch our functional belief tracks, and get the train headed in "whatever" direction is true, honorable, just, pure, lovely, commendable, excellent, or praiseworthy.

This is by no means easy. It's a fight of faith, and fighting is hard, especially if we're out of practice or have never really made this a consistent practice. We should expect it to be difficult. The most wonderful, worthwhile things usually are.

But God is faithful, and this is one of the ways he has provided us an escape from the common-to-mankind temptation to dwell on sinful thought (1 Cor. 10:13). And if we take his escape, he will be faithful to help us "think about these things."

PRAYER

Father, thank you for Paul's gracious exhortation and the escape you provide me through it from remaining in the misery of a sinful train of thought. Give me grace today to query any sinful governing emotion so I can identify and address the underlying sinful functional belief giving rise to any sinful thought pattern. In Jesus' name, amen.

MEDITATE MORE

Review Philippians 4:4–8 to see the connection between escaping anxiety and cultivating godly thoughts.

Jesus' Loving Design in Your Disappointing Church

GOD IS FAITHFUL . . . TO DESIGN THE CHURCH TO DISPLAY THE CALVARY LOVE OF JESUS

Jesus did not design the church to be a place where our dreams come true. Actually, it's a place where many of our dreams are disappointed, which is more of a grace to us than we may realize. Rather, Jesus designed the church to be a place where his love comes true, where there are so many opportunities for us to lay down our lives for each other that the love of Christ becomes a public spectacle.

According to the New Testament, a church's success is not measured by the number of its attenders, the size of its budget, the excellence of its event production, or the scope of its public influence. Its success is measured by the quality of its love. Churches that succeed most as witnesses of Jesus in the world are ones whose members:

- honor one another (Rom. 12:10)
- contribute to meet each other's needs (Rom. 12:13)
- show hospitality to one another (Rom. 12:13)
- rejoice over each other's joys and weep over each other's griefs (Rom. 12:15)
- pursue harmony with each other in spite of differences (Rom. 12:16)
- don't exclude their lowliest brothers or sisters (Rom. 12:16)
- submit to each other (Eph. 5:21)
- persistently strive for agreement over difficult issues (2 Cor. 13:11)
- use their individual freedom in Christ to serve each other (Gal. 5:13)
- bear with each other's many weaknesses (Eph. 4:2)
- forgive each other's sins (Col. 3:13)

- encourage each other to press on in Jesus' mission of love (Heb. 10:24)
- regularly meet together to do all these things (Heb. 10:25)

And what provides the members of such churches the opportunities to express such love? Their inequitable giftings, financial hardships, sacrifices of privacy, grievous losses, vigorous disagreements, various disabilities, yielding authority to others, sacrificing personal rights and preferences, enduring others' irritating and aggravating characteristics, and being hurt by others' sins.

Jesus designed the church to be communities of love—the kind of sacrificial love that's only possible if its members truly believe that God is real, sin is real, Christ's sacrifice is real, the promise of heaven is real, and the threat of hell is real. And he gave the church a mission it can only achieve if its members truly believe that of all the great things they could excel at, "the greatest of these is love" (1 Cor. 13:13).

That's why when it comes to being a member of a church in this age, the community we should envision is not one where we will see our dreams of utopian harmony come true, but one where we will experience true Calvary love. Because in living life together, we "die every day" (1 Cor. 15:31). Central to the mission Jesus gave us to be his witnesses in the world is laying down our lives for each other.

Jesus said, "By this all people will know that you are my disciples, if you have love for one another" (John 13:35). And by intentionally designing our churches to be graciously disappointing communities, he is being true to his word. He's giving us the incredible privilege of and plethora of opportunities for loving our fellow disciples like Jesus loved us—warts and all.

PRAYER

Father, forgive me for all the times I've resented and neglected the church communities you've placed me in that you intended as opportunities for me to love my brothers and sisters as Jesus loved me. Help me see my church with new eyes and give me the grace to experience and display the love of Jesus by faithfully seizing the opportunities you give me today. In Jesus' name, amen.

MEDITATE MORE

Spend time dwelling on 1 Corinthians 13:7: "Love bears all things, believes all things, hopes all things, endures all things." What specific implications do you discern from the Holy Spirit?

88

There was a man named Simon, who had previously practiced magic in the city and amazed the people of Samaria, saying that he himself was somebody great. They all paid attention to him, from the least to the greatest, saying, "This man is the power of God that is called Great." ACTS 8:9–10

God's Gifts Are Not for Our Tiny Greatness

God Is Faithful . . . to Warn You Not to Use His Grace to Enhance Your Reputation

Simon was a local celebrity in his Samaritan town. He loved his "great" reputation and fed off the public's admiration. Then one day Philip showed up. He preached the gospel, and the Holy Spirit came with power, performing signs and wonders through Philip beyond anything Simon had conjured. Large numbers of Samaritans professed faith in Christ and were baptized, including Simon.

Soon Peter and John arrived and joyfully helped nurture this revival. Simon watched in awe as the apostles prayed and Samaritans were filled with the Holy Spirit. The crowds got bigger, and everyone was talking about the great power of God.

But they weren't talking about Simon anymore. His star had been eclipsed. And like many who have experienced the euphoric drug of other people's admiration, Simon wanted that rush again. So, at a discreet moment, he offered Peter and John a small fortune if they would deal him a fix of the Holy Spirit.

Peter immediately discerned Simon's sinful addiction to the drug of *tiny greatness*—the intoxicating pride of being seen as comparatively superior to others and therefore admired and envied by others. Peter knew its seductive power from experience and how spiritually dangerous it is (see Luke 9:46–48; 22:24–27). So, he mercifully minced no words with Simon:

> "May your silver perish with you, because you thought you could obtain the gift of God with money! You have neither part nor lot in this matter, for your heart is not right before God. Repent, therefore, of this

wickedness of yours, and pray to the Lord that, if possible, the intent of your heart may be forgiven you. For I see that you are in the gall of bitterness and in the bond of iniquity." (Acts 8:20–23)

The Holy Spirit, through Peter's rebuke, was faithfully warning Simon of the danger his desire for tiny greatness posed. He was witnessing the great power of God, but his pride was blinding him to its true value. Instead, what he saw was how God, the gospel, the gifts of the Holy Spirit, the apostles, and his fellow townspeople could become means to revive his tiny greatness so he could become "the great power of God" again.

Through Simon's story the Holy Spirit is faithfully warning us too, because we are all tempted by the intoxicating pride of tiny greatness. Many have succumbed to it and used godliness for means to worldly gain (1 Tim. 6:5)—the gain of wealth and status the world admires and envies. But that's not what "the gift of God" is for.

God's "inexpressible gift" is his free grace, which he makes abound to us so that "having all sufficiency in all things at all times, [we'll] abound in every good work," "enriched in every way to be generous in every way, which through us will produce thanksgiving to God" (2 Cor. 9:8–11).

God is faithful when he warns us not to use his gift to achieve tiny greatness for ourselves. For the gift of God is the grace of God given to the people of God so they will experience fullness of joy in God to the glory of God. That's why Jesus tells us, "Freely you have received; freely give" (Matt. 10:8 NIV).

PRAYER

Father, I receive your sober warning through Simon's example, and forgive me for ever using your grace-gifts to enhance my reputation. Today, help me freely give what I have freely received from you in such a way that you receive glory from the way I and others enjoy your grace. In Jesus' name, amen.

MEDITATE MORE

Read 1 Timothy 6:2–10 to see what happens to those who sinfully use God's grace for their worldly gain.

89

So teach us to number our days that we may get a heart of wisdom.

PSALM 90:12

Your Life Is Short: Live Wisely

GOD IS FAITHFUL . . . TO TEACH YOU THE IMPORTANCE OF NUMBERING YOUR DAYS

A few years ago, while visiting my mother, I sifted through some old greeting cards my grandfather had given to my grandmother almost ninety years ago. They were carefully and affectionately preserved because they recall a time when the tender love Roland and Esther shared was very significant to them.

But that time is long past. The number of us who personally witnessed their faithful love shared over sixty years of marriage are few and dwindling. It won't be long before it passes out of living memory.

Life is very short. It won't be long before we too are gone and scant traces of what was so meaningful to us will remain. In view of that, how should we live? Moses' prayer in the verse above tells us we should want to live wisely.

But what does that mean? Providing one answer to that question is the gift of the entire prayer of Moses captured in Psalm 90.

Moses reminds us that the life of God is "from everlasting to everlasting" (v. 2), but our earthly lives are comparable to grass, which flourishes in the morning and withers in the evening (vv. 5–6). If God is eternal and our earthly lives are so ephemeral, then there is only one place the wise will choose to live: in God, who will be for us an eternal dwelling place (v. 1).

Moses reminds us, as Jesus does, that in this world we will have tribulation (John 16:33). If our fleeting, grasslike lives are full of "toil and trouble" (Ps. 90:10), then there is only one ultimate, enduring satisfaction the wise will pursue: the steadfast love of the everlasting God (v. 14).

And Moses reminds us that death is God's judgment on us for our sins. If God brings us to an earthly end because of his righteous wrath (vv. 7–8), and death will come sooner than we think (v. 10), then there is only one thing the wise will seek during this brief terrestrial sojourn: God's mercy and favor (vv. 13, 17).

That's why Moses asks God to "teach us to number our days that we may get a heart of wisdom" (v. 12). Daily numbering our days—recalling how increasingly few of them we have—is one effective way "the fear of the LORD [instructs us] in wisdom" (Prov. 15:33), because it helps us frame our lives in the proper perspective. For we can only live wisely if we remain mindful of who God is and who we are, and view life from God's wide perspective and not our very narrow one.

A number of years ago, I committed Psalm 90 to memory as a way to help me number my days. I commend this to you—it's a short psalm, so it's very doable. Memorize it and make it part of your regular prayers. You'll find that God will faithfully use Moses' prayer as an answer to what Moses prayed: to teach you to number your days so that you'll live wisely.

Someday, sooner than you think, your earthly life will disappear from living memory. As Jesus said to Martha, "You are anxious and troubled about many things, but one thing is necessary." If, like Mary, you choose "the good portion, [it] will not be taken away from [you]" (Luke 10:41–42). Life is short; live wisely.

PRAYER

Father, teach me to number my days, that I may get a heart of wisdom. In Jesus' name, amen.

MEDITATE MORE

Pray through Psalm 90.

Teach Me Your Way, O Lord

GOD IS FAITHFUL . . . TO TEACH YOU HIS WAYS THROUGH EXPERIENCING HIS WAYS

A soldier who has received excellent instruction from highly experienced, decorated warriors, and who has read widely and become impressively knowledgeable about the histories, theories, and strategies of war and the techniques of fighting, but who has had limited personal experience on the actual field of battle, hasn't really learned to fight. He's learned *about* fighting. A soldier never truly learns to fight until he is forced to actually do it. And on the field, he discovers that the experiential knowledge of fighting looks and feels very different from the abstract knowledge of it.

The same is true for disciples of Jesus. A disciple can gain an impressive amount of knowledge about the life of faith through studying the experience of other highly experienced, deeply knowledgeable, profoundly godly disciples. But he never truly learns the ways of God and how to walk by faith and not by sight (2 Cor. 5:7) until he is forced to actually do it. And on the field, he discovers that the experiential knowledge of living by faith looks and feels very different from the abstract knowledge of it.

That's why when we sincerely pray with David, "Teach me your way, O LORD" (Ps. 27:11), and God answers us, which he's faithful to do, his answers often look and feel very different from what we thought we were asking for.

We learn so much about the ways of God from David. We see them play out in the scriptural histories of David's life, and we especially see them in the psalms David wrote. But David learned the ways of God on the field of experience that inspired those psalms. And those experiences were often chaotic, disorienting, disturbing, and violent. David learned the most about God's ways and how to trust them, and how to put his faith in God's promises and not his own perceptions, in the places of his desperation where he was forced to do so. It was in the crucible of these hard situations that he really learned how to pray and what it means to truly worship God.

The psalms of David that we love were David's poetic processing of how to put his hope and joy in God in the face of overwhelming circumstances. They are fruit God produced through David as God taught him his ways, and they have nourished and encouraged the faith of, and consoled and given worshipful, prayerful voice to God's children for thousands of years.

But as much as we can learn from David's experience about living by faith, we can never truly learn to live by faith until we, like him, are forced to actually do it.

Disciples learn the ways of their masters, so they become like their masters—that's what it means to be a disciple. We have become disciples of Jesus because we want to learn his ways and become like him. We say to him, "Teach me your ways, O LORD." And he says to us, "Follow me" (Luke 5:27). And he leads us into places most conducive for our learning: the difficult, often desperate places that force us to exercise faith in him.

But as we learn Jesus' ways, these desperate places become precious places. Because these are where we, like David, experientially learn that God is faithful to his promises and that his "steadfast love is better than life" (Ps. 63:3).

PRAYER

Father, teach me your ways! I don't want to merely know about you, I want to truly know you and your Son and your Spirit. I want the full sweetness of knowing your steadfast love that is better than life. So, lead me to the places most conducive to my truly learning. In Jesus' name, amen.

MEDITATE MORE

Read Psalm 27. What was David learning about the ways of God?

Jesus' Mercy on Those Who Doubt

GOD IS FAITHFUL . . . TO SHOW US HOW TO HAVE MERCY
ON THOSE STRUGGLING WITH DOUBT

According to tradition, the person who penned these words was Jesus' brother. And I can't help thinking that their roots went back to a time when Jude doubted his divine brother's claims (John 7:5) and Jesus had mercy on him.

Jesus set a faithful example, not only with Jude, but with numerous others, of how to have mercy on those who doubt, and how different kinds of doubts call for different kinds of mercy.

One touching example comes from Matthew 11:2–6. John the Baptist was languishing in Herod's prison and knew he was likely headed to execution. We can only imagine the spiritual oppression and emotional distress that caused him to second-guess if he'd prophesied accurately about Jesus. So, through his disciples, John asked Jesus, "Are you the one who is to come, or shall we look for another?" (Matt. 11:3). Jesus' response was merciful kindness, intended to fortify his faithful friend in his final brutal days, not break him when he was a bruised reed (Matt. 12:20). *There's a gentle mercy for those who doubt in the darkness of suffering and isolation.*

Another example comes from Matthew 14:28–33. Peter had just exercised significant faith in Jesus by getting out of the boat to walk on top of the stormy sea. But when fear began to grow, his faith began to shrink, and Jesus let him sink. This prompted Peter to cry for Jesus' help, which he received along with this rebuke: "O you of little faith, why did you doubt?" (v. 31). Jesus' response was merciful disappointment, intended to imprint upon Peter (and the others) the danger of transferring his trust from the power of the Word to the power of the world. *There's a firm mercy for those who doubt in fearful situations that demand focused, persevering faith.*

A third example comes from John 20:24–29. Thomas was the only disciple left who didn't claim to have seen the risen Jesus. It didn't matter what Jesus had previously promised, what trusted eyewitnesses claimed, or that the tomb was empty. In the face of the fierce reality of Jesus' brutal death, Thomas declared, "Unless I . . . place my finger into the mark of the nails, and place my hand into his side, I will never believe" (John 20:25). Jesus' response was merciful delay. He let Thomas sit in his unbelief for eight miserable, lonely days. And then, when the time was right, Jesus appeared to him, saying, "Do not disbelieve, but believe" (John 20:27). *There's a disciplining mercy for those who doubt because they elevate their wisdom above God's* (1 Cor. 1:25).

These three examples are just a sampling of the many varieties of doubt people experience. But they give us glimpses of different ways Jesus faithfully extended mercy to those who experienced different kinds of doubts. And they are a few of the ways God faithfully shows us how we, like Jude, can follow in Jesus' merciful footsteps.

PRAYER

Father, thank you for how often you have had mercy on me and faithfully pursued me when I've battled my various doubts. Give me both grace and wisdom as I seek to extend the kind of mercy the doubting person most needs. In Jesus' name, amen.

MEDITATE MORE

Read the three accounts given above where Jesus showed mercy to his doubting friends. Who in your life is struggling with doubt? What would your having mercy on them look like?

> *Therefore, since we are surrounded by so great a cloud of witnesses, let us also lay aside every weight, and sin which clings so closely, and let us run with endurance the race that is set before us.*
>
> HEBREWS 12:1

Embrace the Race God Gives You

GOD IS FAITHFUL ... TO TEACH YOU HOW TO RUN THE RACE HE'S SET BEFORE YOU

You have a race to run. It's a race God has given you, not one you've chosen. It's possible you wouldn't have chosen your race at all, had the choice been yours. But here you are: in this race, on this route, at this pace, on this terrain, in this climate, with these people, with your strengths, with your limitations, for this distance. You may not have chosen your race, but you do get to choose how you run it.

But you don't have to figure it out on your own. The author of Hebrews gives you some expert running advice.

Learn from other great runners. If you want to run well, study other runners. Hebrews 11 provides a helpful starter list, but it is by no means exhaustive. Study the great faith-runners. Examine all aspects of their courses. God did far more abundantly than all they asked or thought (Eph. 3:20). He will faithfully do more for you too, if you run faithfully.

Run as light as possible. We each bring to our unique races our unique temperaments, upbringings, conditioned habits, cultural expectations, hopes, dreams, fears, and familiar sins. Some of these are provisions from God for the race set before us. But some are unnecessary weights and hindering sins that pull you down, and these need to be let go of and laid aside. All the other great runners have had them too and we can learn from their example how to lay them aside. Focus on your race, and only carry what God gives you—and his burden is light (Matt. 11:30).

Run with endurance. Endurance is only increased by pushing against our current limits. And pushing beyond where we feel we can go is hard. In the intense discomfort of this experience, you will often feel like you'll never be able to run like other great faith-runners. But that's also how they felt when they were building endurance. So today, push against today's limits. When tomorrow comes, push against tomorrow's limits. What exhausts you today will be much easier in the future, but then you'll be pushing different limits. Beware of comparing yourself to other great faith-runners. Let Jesus make you into whatever runner he wants. Focus on faithfully and prayerfully increasing your current endurance for your race.

Keep your eyes on the prize. Look to Jesus. He is your Savior, your greatest faith-race example and your greatest intercessor (Heb. 7:25). He is the source of your greatest joy, your one great prize for running well (Ps. 16:11; John 15:11). You aren't just running your race to enhance your spiritual health; you are running to win a prize. If the prize is not before your eyes, you will lose motivation. Keep your eyes on the Prize and "run that you may obtain it" (1 Cor. 9:24).

This is your race. God has set it before you and has faithfully provided you many means of grace to help you run faithfully. Study the great faith-runners, run as light as possible, push your current endurance limits, and keep your eyes on the Great Prize. Run freer, run faster, and run for joy—the joy set before you.

PRAYER

Father, thank you for the race you have set before me, and for all the graces you have provided to help me run in faith, and that you promise to always be with me (Matt. 28:20) and supply me the strength I need (1 Peter 4:11). Help me today to learn from others, to lay aside weights and sins, increase my endurance, and look to Jesus, my great example and great Prize. In Jesus' name, amen.

MEDITATE MORE

Review Hebrews 11 to look for examples of how others learned to run their race by faith.

Why Are You Afraid?

GOD IS FAITHFUL . . . TO DELIVER YOU FROM
YOUR GREATEST DANGER

There are a lot of frightening things in the world. And evil, fearful things befall Christians. Is it possible to not fear them? And didn't Jesus teach us to pray, "Deliver us from evil" (Matt. 6:13)? Isn't God supposed to be "a refuge for us" from the things we most fear (Ps. 62:8)? If God does not spare us from these sorts of fearful evils, then what sort of a refuge is he? In what way does he deliver us from evil?

These are questions we must come to terms with if we are to endure evil's onslaught with our faith intact. For we will not put our faith in a God we do not trust. And we will not trust a God who promises to protect us and isn't true to his word.

But the fundamental question for each of us is not, "God, will you protect me from my worst fears?" Rather, it's Jesus' question to us: "Why are you afraid?" (Matt. 8:26). Jesus asks all of us this question because he knows we all have disordered fears. Our worst fears are often not focused on our greatest dangers. And God has faithfully designed fear to tell us what we believe our true dangers are and where true safety is found. He designed fear to tell us what we most fear to lose, because that tells us where we derive our greatest hope.

So, it's important to keep in mind what kinds of evil Jesus promises to faithfully deliver us from and what kind of safe refuge God promises to faithfully be for us.

The Bible reveals that what poses us the greatest danger is God's holy and just wrath against our sin (Rom. 5:6–9). Sin is a great danger because it threatens us with the loss of the greatest Treasure in existence: God. And it can result in our experiencing the worst misery possible: the eternal judgment of God.

The primary reason Jesus came was to deliver us from our greatest danger by removing the guilt of sin from all who put their faith in him, thus removing them from the danger of God's righteous judgment. In doing this, Jesus becomes the greatest refuge from the greatest danger we face.

But in doing this, Jesus also ultimately becomes the great refuge from every danger, period. For he came to ultimately and completely "destroy the works of the devil" (1 John 3:8) and ultimately "rescue [us] from every evil deed and bring [us] safely into his heavenly kingdom" (2 Tim. 4:18).

But the Bible makes clear that in this age, we do not yet experience Jesus' total deliverance from all evil, which means there are plenty of frightening things, like tribulation, distress, persecution, famine, nakedness, danger, and swords (Rom. 8:35). But when Peter tells us not to "fear anything that is frightening," he doesn't mean we won't experience them as fearful. He means we're not to fear them more than our greatest danger, because if we do, we will take sinful actions to escape them and thereby put ourselves in greater danger.

So, Jesus faithfully asks you, "What are you afraid of?" It's a merciful question because he wants you to seek your ultimate refuge in him. And if you do, no frightening thing will ever separate you from the eternal refuge that is his steadfast love (Rom. 8:35).

PRAYER

Father, thank you for so mercifully providing me the refuge of your Son from the greatest danger I could ever face. Help me more clearly see the danger sin poses to me so that I never fear a less frightening thing more than I fear being separated from you. In Jesus' name, amen.

MEDITATE MORE

Review Romans 8:31–39.

94 | *May the God of hope fill you with all joy and peace in believing, so that by the power of the Holy Spirit you may abound in hope.*

ROMANS 15:13

Why You Can't Live by Bread Alone

GOD IS FAITHFUL . . . TO GIVE YOUR SOUL WHAT IT NEEDS TO LIVE AND FLOURISH

This beautiful blessing from the apostle Paul describes in one sentence the state of mind that provides us the greatest mental health. I don't mean "mental health" in the clinical sense, as some conditions require serious medical treatment. Rather, I'm referring to the general state of mind that makes for optimal human flourishing. And that state of mind is *abounding in hope.*

When we're hopeful, the world is full of wonder and possibilities. We have drive and curiosity. We tackle challenges and strive to overcome adversity. But when we run low on hope, the world becomes a fearful, threatening place. A hope deficit saps our desire and drive, it robs us of interest and appetite. It makes us want to retreat in order to protect our inner selves, what the Bible calls our souls.

God designed our souls to run on hope, just like he made our outer selves, our bodies, to run on energy. Like our bodies grow faint when we run low on energy, our souls grow faint when we run low on hope. So, when our bodies need energy we eat food, which our bodies digest and convert into energy. But when our souls need hope, what do we feed them? Promises. A promise is "soul food" that we digest by "believing" and is converted into hope.

Hope is what we feel about the future, which means we have hope if we believe our future is promising. So, we feed on promises. That's why God tells us, "Man does not live by bread alone, but . . . by every word that comes from the mouth of the LORD" (Deut. 8:3; quoted by Jesus in Matt. 4:4). He designed our souls to be nourished by his "precious and very great promises"

(2 Peter 1:4). Or put another way, he designed us to live by faith in all future graces he promises to provide us.

But as we can derive energy by feeding our bodies junk food, we can derive hope by feeding our souls junk promises. And like junk food's bad effects on bodily health, junk promises produce the kinds of hope that keep us going for the short run, but they're bad for our soul's mental health, because they can lead to soul-diseases and even soul-death.

In order to abound in the kind of hope that fills us with "all joy and peace" and leads to our optimal, long-term flourishing, we need promises God designed to nourish our souls so we can live and serve "by the strength that God supplies" (1 Peter 4:11). And God faithfully supplies us an inexhaustible storehouse of the promises our souls most need in his word. These promises are "living and active" (Heb. 4:12), proceeding directly from the living Word, Jesus Christ (John 1:1), in whom "all the promises of God find their Yes" (2 Cor. 1:20).

This is why Jesus called himself "the bread of life" (John 6:35). Only in believing in him, and all he promises to be and do for you, can the God of hope fill you with all joy and peace in believing, so that by the power of the Holy Spirit you may abound in hope. "If anyone eats of this bread, he will live forever" (John 6:51).

PRAYER

Father, thank you for faithfully providing my soul the food it most needs so that I may abound in hope—especially the Bread of life. Yes, Lord, "give [me] this bread always" (John 6:34)! In Jesus' name, amen.

MEDITATE MORE

Read John 6:22–51 and feed on "the bread of God . . . who [came] down from heaven and gives life to the world" (John 6:33).

> *O God, you are my God; earnestly I seek you; my soul thirsts for you; my flesh faints for you, as in a dry and weary land where there is no water.* PSALM 63:1

The Blessedness of the Barren Places

GOD IS FAITHFUL . . . WHEN HE LEADS YOU INTO SEASONS OF SPIRITUAL DEPRIVATION

What David captures here in beautiful poetic verse is the blessedness of the spiritually barren places. "Blessed" and "barren" aren't words that typically go together. Let me explain what I mean by expounding on the experience of finding "no water."

When water is always available and you can gratify your slightest tinge of thirst anytime you wish, how intensely do you appreciate your need of water? How earnestly do you seek it? Now, what about when you are very thirsty, and no water is accessible? Then how much do you appreciate your need of it, and how earnestly do you seek it?

The thirstier you are, the more aware you become of water's immense value. You realize how much you need it, and how much it satisfies you. And when you've been deprived of water for an uncomfortable period of time and finally get a drink, you enjoy its life-sustaining refreshment in a way you don't when you can take it for granted. In fact, the heightened pleasure water gives you when it quenches your deep thirst can make you feel grateful for the experience of its deprivation.

Our experience of spiritually dry and weary lands produces similar effects. God leads us into seasons of various kinds of experiential spiritual deprivation, which awakens in us a more intense awareness of how much we need the life-sustaining refreshment and hope he provides. And our need moves us to seek him more earnestly. And when we've been experientially deprived of him for an uncomfortable, unpleasant period of time, and then finally "taste and see" his goodness (Ps. 34:8), we enjoy him in ways we don't when his graces are so experientially accessible that we take them for granted. In fact, the heightened pleasure in God we experience when he quenches our deep soul-thirst makes us feel grateful for whatever deprivation we experienced.

This is the blessedness of the spiritually barren places. It is one way we experience our Father's loving, faithful discipline. "For the moment all discipline seems painful rather than pleasant, but later it yields the peaceful fruit of righteousness to those who have been trained by it" (Heb. 12:11). And the peaceful fruit born in the barren places is righteous, holy desire.

"God is most glorified in us when we are most satisfied in him."[33] But we only seek our satisfaction most in God when God is what we desire most. And when, due to our living in a fallen world with natures still infected with remaining sin, our awareness becomes dulled by too much abundance, God mercifully and faithfully brings us to some spiritually "dry and weary land where there is no water" to intensify and deepen our awareness of our need for him and reawaken and deepen our desire for him.

It is a painful rather than pleasant experience. But later, when the barren land has done its redemptive, thirst-provoking work, God will refresh us again with his "living water" (John 7:38), and we will thank him for the profound gift of experiencing the blessedness of our barren place.

PRAYER

Father, my soul thirsts for you. But I am often aware of how dull this thirst can be. In your wisdom, faithfully lead me to whatever "dry and weary land" I need, that through my thirst I may remember how much I need you and experience the satisfaction only you provide when I drink deeply of the "spring of the water of life" (Rev. 21:6). In Jesus' name, amen.

MEDITATE MORE

Read Psalm 42. What need did the psalmist's "thirst for God" awaken?

96

For the love of money is a root of all kinds of evils. It is through this craving that some have wandered away from the faith and pierced themselves with many pangs. 1 TIMOTHY 6:10

The Secret of Facing Abundance

GOD IS FAITHFUL . . . TO SHOW YOU HOW TO ESCAPE THE DANGERS OF LOVING MONEY

Paul's word to Timothy here is one of many faithful warnings God gives us to flee from financial immorality. I'm adapting Paul's phrase, "Flee from sexual immorality" (1 Cor. 6:18), and I don't think he'd have any disagreement.

Neither would Jesus, who more often spoke to the dangers of money than the dangers of misusing sex. And his warnings were more dire. For example, Jesus didn't say it's harder for a sexually immoral person to get into heaven than a camel to squeeze through a needle's eye; he said it about rich people (Mark 10:24–25).

I say this, not to diminish the very real dangers of sexual sin (1 Cor. 6:9–11), but to increase our awareness of the dangers of financial sin, especially because most Christians in my nation are far wealthier than almost anyone Jesus or Paul addressed. Yet there are many times more sermons and resources devoted to help Christians escape sexual sin than financial sin.

Given the things Jesus and Paul said about the spiritual dangers of loving money, you'd think we prosperous Christians would be forming accountability groups like crazy to help us keep our lives free from the love of money (Heb. 13:5). We know that too much exposure to sexually immoral images and the seductive promises sexual temptation makes can easily desensitize us to their dangers. But we are even more pervasively exposed to the images and promises financial sin makes to us. We need to ask how this has affected us. How desensitized are we to the dangers of loving and serving money? Because Jesus said we "cannot serve God and money" (Luke 16:13).

Paul wrote something remarkably helpful in a letter he wrote from prison: "I have learned the secret of facing plenty and hunger, abundance and need. I can do all things through him who strengthens me" (Phil. 4:12–13).

He speaks of "facing" abundance in the same way he speaks of "facing" need. In other words, Paul had to learn how to exercise faith in the face of both, because both present temptations to sin.

Financial abundance tempts us through its deceptive promises of security, autonomy, cultural prestige, and privilege, as well as the indulgent opportunities it affords. It frees us from many discomforts that come with being in need. But according to Jesus, we are completely needy, as needy as a branch is of its vine (John 15:5). And this is why, for most people, material abundance is spiritually harder to face faithfully than material need. Because material abundance is more likely to obscure our spiritual need, whereas material need is more likely to expose our spiritual need.

But there is a secret to faithfully facing the powerful temptations of abundance, the secret Paul learned. It lies in believing the promise that "God is able to make all grace abound to you, so that having all sufficiency in all things at all times, you may abound in every good work" (2 Cor. 9:8). If you believe the promise that God will faithfully "supply every need of yours according to his riches in glory in Christ Jesus" (Phil. 4:19), you can face abundance without being seduced by it and escape the many pangs that afflict those who fall in love with it.

PRAYER

Father, I confess that I am not as frightened as I should be of the dangers of the love of money. But I don't want to be seduced by it, wander away from the faith, and be pierced with the resulting terrible pangs. Teach me the secret of faithfully facing both abundance and need, for I can do all things through the strength that you provide. In Jesus' name, amen.

MEDITATE MORE

Read Mark 10:17–31 where Jesus shows us the danger of the love of money and gives us hope for how to escape it.

97

"For where your treasure is, there your heart will be also."

MATTHEW 6:21

Your Pleasures Never Lie

GOD IS FAITHFUL . . . IN MAKING YOUR PLEASURE THE MEASURE OF YOUR TREASURE

Jesus reveals something gloriously wonderful and devastating in this brief but crucial teaching on treasuring.

What's gloriously wonderful is that God blatantly entices us to seek our happiness, joy, pleasure—whatever you want to call it—*in him*. Of course, I'm not basing this on these verses alone. Throughout Scripture, God holds himself out to us as our most valuable treasure (Matt. 13:44–45), supreme delight (Ps. 37:4), greatest gain (Phil. 3:8–9), highest reward (Heb. 11:6), fullest joy, and longest-lasting pleasure (Ps. 16:11). And the reason he does is because God wants us to pursue our pleasure.

Why does God want us to pursue our pleasure? Because he designed it to function as a crucial indicator. Pleasure is the meter in your heart that measures how valuable, how precious, someone or something is to you. *Pleasure is the measure of your treasure.* And you "glorify" the worth of your treasure by how much pleasure it gives you.

That's what Jesus is getting at here. You treasure what you love. What you treasure most is what most captures your heart. Therefore, God wants you to treasure him, because "*God is most glorified in [you] when [you] are most satisfied in him.*"[34]

That's wonderful news for us! God is not indifferent about our joy; he wants us to have the most joy possible.

But here's the devastating side of Jesus' teaching. If pleasure is the measure of your treasure, then pleasure becomes your heart's whistle-blower if you treasure something or someone more than God. Because,

The soul is measured by its flights,
Some low and others high.
The heart is known by its delights,
And pleasures never lie.[35]

This is an exposing truth. It can be devastating to stand before God with disordered, sinful pleasures revealing the state of our hearts. But it is a merciful devastation we desperately need. For we must know our spiritual poverty before we will earnestly seek true spiritual wealth. We must see our miserable idolatries before we will repent and forsake them. We must feel our spiritual deadness before we will cry out, "Will you not revive us again, that your people may rejoice in you?" (Ps. 85:6).

God created pleasure because he is a happy God and wants his joy to be in us and our joy to be full (John 15:11). His ultimate purpose in designing pleasure as the measure of our treasure is that we would experience maximal joy in the supreme Treasure, and the Treasure would receive maximal glory from our joy in him. It is a marvelous and merciful design, even if our pleasures reveal the devastating truth that the Treasure is not our treasure. Because then the Spirit can convict us of our idolatrous love and we can repent and return to the Treasure who is "faithful and just to forgive us our sins and to cleanse us from all unrighteousness" (1 John 1:9).

If God has to expose our poverty to pursue our eternal prosperity, he will. But it comes from his heart's desire that we experience "fullness of joy" in his presence and "pleasures forevermore" at his right hand (Ps. 16:11). He wants our hearts captured by the true Treasure. So, it's a great, and at times devastating, mercy that our pleasures never lie.

PRAYER

Father, once more I am awed at the wisdom with which you made me. Your design in my pleasure is fearful and wonderful (Ps. 139:14). I confess that I am a mixed bag of passions, and my simple prayer is that you'd forgive me for any idolatrous loves and do whatever it takes to help me treasure you supremely so that my heart is with you. I want you to receive eternal glory from my forever pleasure in you. In Jesus' name, amen.

MEDITATE MORE

Read Luke 19:1–10 to watch a glorious treasure transfer take place.

98 *Whom have I in heaven but you? And there is nothing on earth that I desire besides you. My flesh and my heart may fail, but God is the strength of my heart and my portion forever.* PSALM 73:25-26

Your Portion Forever

GOD IS FAITHFUL . . . TO SHOW YOU THAT HE IS
THE HEAVEN YOU LONG FOR

These verses are all about heaven, even though the author says nothing specific about heaven except that without God, heaven is nothing to him. Which is precisely my point. If heaven is where our souls will experience the satisfaction we long for in our heart of hearts, then a heaven without God is no heaven at all. For God is what makes heaven heavenly. He is the Heaven of heaven.

In the same way these verses are all about heaven, the Bible is a book all about heaven, though it says surprisingly little about heaven *the place*. The few vivid descriptions of heaven it contains are full of confusing symbols and analogical imagery drawn from the ancient world its original readers inhabited, but quite strange to us. It leaves us with an unclear idea of heaven, and yet it doesn't. For the Bible is full of revelation about God, and he's what makes heaven heavenly. It matters little what heaven *the place* is like as long as God is there. And if he's not, it doesn't matter at all.

This motif carries over into the realm of our desires for heaven. C. S. Lewis wrote, "There have been times when I think we do not desire heaven; but more often I find myself wondering whether, in our heart of hearts, we have ever desired anything else."[36] He's referring to the desire at the core of all our desiring, the thirst that is never quenched by anything we find in this world. Lewis calls it "the secret signature of each soul, the incommunicable and unappeasable want, the thing we desired before we met our wives or made our friends or chose our work, and which we shall still desire on our deathbeds, when the mind no longer knows wife or friend or work."[37]

The "unappeasable want." You have it. I have it. Its presence is pervasive in our pursuits. Yet quenching this thirst eludes us in every earthly well we drink from. For only one thing can quench it: heaven. But not heaven *the place*; Heaven the Person. As Randy Alcorn says,

> We may imagine we want a thousand different things, but God is the one we really long for. His presence brings satisfaction; his absence brings thirst and longing. Our longing for Heaven is a longing for God.[38]

God himself is "the fountain of living waters"; apart from him every other cistern we try to drink from leaves us dry (Jer. 2:13). Only he can give us the drink that will forever end our deepest thirst (John 4:14).

Our unquenchable thirst, our unappeasable want, is our desire for heaven. And our desire for heaven is our desire for the only thing that makes heaven heavenly: God. Even our longing for immortality is a longing for God. For, as Jesus said, "This is eternal life, that they know you, the only true God, and Jesus Christ whom you have sent" (John 17:3). God does not merely give us eternal life; he *is* the life, the very source and essence of eternal life (John 11:25–26). Eternal life apart from God is nothing but a living hell.

The greatest gift we will ever receive from God, the greatest benefit we will ever reap from all his faithful, steadfast love has accomplished for us in Christ, is God himself. He will always only be our "exceeding joy" (Ps. 43:4), our greatest "gain" (Phil. 3:8), and our most satisfying "portion forever" (Ps. 73:26).

PRAYER

Father, whom have I in heaven but you? And there is nothing on earth that I desire besides you. My flesh and my heart may fail, but you are the strength of my heart and my portion forever through Christ. Amen.

MEDITATE MORE

Read John 17 to hear the Heaven of heaven's desire for you.

You, My Friend, Are the Glorious Grass of God

GOD IS FAITHFUL . . . EVEN WHEN YOUR GRASSLIKE LIFE COMES TO AN END

Not long ago, I buried a good friend. Another victim of cancer. Another casualty of the fall. Another reminder of the ignoble prosaic ending to the poem so noble and full of wild glory that neither tongues of men nor angels can fully capture: an ordinary human life.

There actually exists no such thing: an ordinary human life. It is a great misnomer, an oxymoron of colossal proportion. To think of a life as ordinary reveals the shameful fact that we can barely bear true beauty. We tire quickly of sunsets and define boring as watching the grass grow. It's very strange that we find violent virtual deaths in our films more exciting than the gentle life that miraculously awakens when buried, pushes up through the dark soil, catches the sunlight for food, and grows into a brilliantly green brushstroke of beauty in the very real landscape art we view in full 4D every day.

"As for man, his days are like grass" (Ps. 103:15). Perhaps that is why we find the lives of men boring and ordinary: watching a man is like watching the grass grow.

My friend was like grass. But he found the adventure of grass less boring than most of us. He was a farmer. Year after year he tilled the dark soil, buried the seeds, and watched the epic of nourishing life slowly unfold. He endured the suspense and occasional tragedies of storms, droughts, and pestilence. He knew that the flower of the field was both fiercely resilient and fearfully fragile.

My friend was like grass. His life was one of unassuming beauty. In the landscape of humanity, you might not notice him unless you were paying attention. He was gentle and quiet. He moved like the slow, steady rhythms of the seasons. He was poetry in motion. But we, who have largely lost the patience required for poetry, might call it slow motion.

With unpretentious drama he came to faith in the living Christ while young, faithfully loved a faithful wife for forty years, and faithfully raised three children well into adulthood, each child now sharing his faith. And he faithfully shared his faith with anyone willing to listen, and many who weren't. Even in the evening of his life, when his grasslike body was withering, hospice nurses heard about his hope in the bright morning star who makes it possible for us, even though we die, to live in the eternal morning where the grass of God withers no more (Ps. 90:5–6; John 11:25–26; 1 Peter 3:15; Rev. 21:4; 22:16).

My friend was like grass. Grass might seem to grow slowly, but in reality, its poetic life is brief. The scorching wind of cancer passed over him and now he is gone (Ps. 103:16). He suffered the ignoble dishonor of death, and we sowed the perishable remains of this gentle, down-to-earth man, like a seed, into the ground. But make no mistake: we indeed sowed it. For it is the core of the Christian hope, the hope at the core of my friend's very soul, that what is sown perishable will be raised imperishable (1 Cor. 15:42–44).

A day is coming when we will know that the epic story of this quiet, grasslike man has always been far more thrilling than the best novels and the greatest films. And we will marvel that we ever considered such a thing ordinary.

Someday the curse will be reversed, and we will not have the patience to watch the millisecond epics of cinematic mass murder that captured the imagination of fallen man. Not when what is playing out before us in vibrant colors now inconceivable is the gloriously wild, real story of everlasting grass that, having burst from the ground, is alive with the light of the undying Star.

And you, my friend, are also the glorious grass of your faithful God.

PRAYER

Father, that you have given me such hope makes me bow my head in worship. Truly, your steadfast love never ceases, and your mercies never come to an end, even when my earthly life does. For they will still be new when my eternal morning begins. Great is your faithfulness! In Jesus' name, amen.

MEDITATE MORE

Read Revelation 22:1–5. This is the future of the glorious grass of the faithful God.

Next Year in Jerusalem!

GOD WILL FAITHFULLY GIVE YOU YOUR PROMISED EVERLASTING HOME IN AN ETERNAL CITY

Every year the Jewish diaspora end their Passover Seder with this wistful prayer: "Next year in Jerusalem." It expresses the deep longing for the promised Messiah's long-awaited arrival, which will finally bring lasting peace and restored worship to Jerusalem. It is a profound yearning that perhaps next year those who have been strangers and exiles on the earth for so long will finally see an end to their sojourning and return to their promised forever home.

"Next year in Jerusalem!" is what Christians ought to wish each other, perhaps at the closing of each passing year, as we await the Messiah's second arrival. For we too are seeking "the holy city, new Jerusalem," that is to come (Rev. 21:2), where we will at long last know the fullness of joy and peace for which each of us deeply longs.

In this city, "the dwelling place of God [will be] with man. He will dwell with them, and they will be his people, and God himself will be with them as their God," and he will "[make] all things new" (Rev. 21:3, 5).

In this city, God "will wipe away every tear from [our] eyes, and death shall be no more, neither shall there be mourning, nor crying, nor pain anymore, for the former things [will] have passed away," and "no longer will there be anything accursed" (Rev. 21:4; 22:3).

In this city, we will finally realize the end of our incessant earthly restlessness, the healing of the homesickness for that place we've not yet seen, and the dreams we've never been able to adequately describe will come true.

In this city, we will finally worship the triune God with our entire being, in unfiltered glory and in dimensions of spirit and truth that are unimaginable to us now. And we will wonder that we ever used the phrase "joy that is inexpressible and filled with glory" (1 Peter 1:8) during our years of dimmed, muted, sin-impoverishing, defective worship when at last our faith gives way to the sight of this:

> The throne of God and of the Lamb will be in [the city], and his servants will . . . see his face, and his name will be on their foreheads. And night will be no more. They will need no light of lamp or sun, for the Lord God will be their light, and they will reign forever and ever. (Rev. 22:3–5)

Alas! Now we still find ourselves peering into the dark glass (1 Cor. 13:12), still experiencing tribulation (John 16:33), still hearing of "wars and rumors of wars" (Matt. 24:6), still walking "by faith, not by sight" (2 Cor. 5:7). We still find that "here we have no lasting city," we still find ourselves seeking "the city that is to come."

But it will not always be so. Just as the Messiah's long-awaited first coming occurred, his long-awaited second coming will also occur. It will happen "in a moment, in the twinkling of an eye" (1 Cor. 15:52). And it will happen soon, perhaps next year.

May it be, Father! Bring your work to completion and send your Son for his bride! For Jesus promised, "Surely I am coming soon." And we, his bride, all say, "Amen. Come, Lord Jesus!" (Rev. 22:20). Come soon!

"Next year in Jerusalem!"

MEDITATE MORE

Allow this verse to increase your spiritual thirst and fuel your prayers for the fulfillment of all your faithful God has promised you in Christ, your Beloved (Eph. 1:6):

> The Spirit and the Bride say, "Come." And let the one who hears say, "Come." And let the one who is thirsty come; let the one who desires take the water of life without price. (Rev. 22:17)

Gratitude

Jim, my older brother by five years, first became a profound spiritual mentor for me in the fall of 1978, when he was eighteen years old and I, thirteen. The moment is clear because Jim had a transformative encounter with Jesus as college freshman. "Conversion" is the right word; I was an eyewitness of his metamorphosis. I saw Jesus become real to him. I saw him come alive. I saw his affections and interests change. I saw him desire God in a way I, as a spiritually earnest adolescent, longed to desire God. Jim became my first real role model for what it means to be a godly man.

Forty-five years have since passed. Jim and I have gone from teenagers to late middle-agers. We've received our educations, married godly women, raised our children, followed Jesus' call into vocational ministry—Jim, mostly among those whose lives have been damaged by generational poverty and disenfranchisement and all struggles and pain that go with those— and now we can see the end of our sojourns approaching. And Jim is still a role model for me. I have been an eyewitness of his faithfulness in all his callings, and I know that the fiber in Jim's faithfulness is his unswerving faith in the faithfulness of God—that God will be true to his word.

Thank you, Jim, for all your faithful life has meant to me. And the priceless gift of counting you among my dearest friends. Dedicating this book to you is a very small expression of my gratitude for you.

Pervasive throughout these meditations are the passionate, worshipful, theological, stylistic, tonal, and editorial influences of my teaching colleagues at Desiring God: John Piper, David Mathis, Marshall Segal, Scott Hubbard, Greg Morse, and Joe Rigney. All that is good in this book has been shaped by this remarkable fellowship of writers. All that is deficient is my own fault.

Thank you to my friend, Trillia Newbell, for inviting me to write this book for Moody Publishers, to Pamela Pugh for improving it through her editorial skill, and for the patient team at Moody for graciously publishing it.

More thanks than anyone else knows goes to my wife, Pam. Due to unforeseen circumstances, she made it possible for me to finish this book in a time frame far more condensed than we had planned. And she frequently strengthened my heart by her confidence in God's faithfulness and her patience with me.

Finally, thank you, Father, for being true to your word. These meditations are the result of my trusting your word for nearly fifty years, and all the praying, pondering, wrestling, marveling, doubting, rejoicing, and enduring this has involved. You've led me through seasons in green pastures and through seasons in valleys of deep darkness (Ps. 23:2–4). Whatever my lot, you have taught me to say:

> The steadfast love of the LORD never ceases;
>> his mercies never come to an end;
> they are new every morning;
>> great is your faithfulness. (Lam. 3:22–23)

Amen. You are my portion; therefore I will hope in you (Lam. 3:24).

Notes

1. Don Phillips, "NTSB Says Disorientation Likely Caused JFK Jr. Crash," *Washington Post*, July 7, 2000, https://www.washingtonpost.com/archive/politics/2000/07/07/ntsb-says-disorientation-likely-caused-jfk-jr-crash/08cd60a8-74ae-46e1-a2e8-960ab2e71116/.

2. I share in more detail one "spiritual storm" I experienced in this article, "When Your Worst Storm Comes," *Desiring God*, July 16, 2019, https://www.desiringgod.org/articles/when-your-worst-storm-comes.

3. Smithsonian Channel, "Does This Scenario Explain JFK Jr.'s Plane Crash?," www.youtube.com, January 20, 2017, https://www.youtube.com/watch?v=-P-3Kl1P0as.

4. National Institute of Standards and Technology, "NIST Clock Experiment Demonstrates That Your Head Is Older Than Your Feet," NIST, September 28, 2010, https://www.nist.gov/news-events/news/2010/09/nist-clock-experiment-demonstrates-your-head-older-your-feet.

5. The National Coordination Office for Space-Based Positioning, Navigation, and Timing, "GPS: The Global Positioning System," GPS.gov, 2019, https://www.gps.gov/.

6. Jon Bloom, "Seven Things to Pray for Your Children," *Desiring God*, March 8, 2013, https://www.desiringgod.org/articles/seven-things-to-pray-for-your-children.

7. Annie S. Hawks and Robert Lowry, "I Need Thee Every Hour," 1872, public domain.

8. John Piper, "God Is Always Doing 10,000 Things in Your Life," *Desiring God*, January 1, 2013, https://www.desiringgod.org/articles/god-is-always-doing-10000-things-in-your-life.

9. Tony Reinke, *Newton on the Christian Life: To Live Is Christ* (Wheaton, IL: Crossway, 2015), 220.

10. Ibid., 222.

11. Ibid., 221.

12. Ibid., 234.

13. There are numerous differing versions of this legend. My retelling was most shaped by summaries located (as of 07/06/2022) at https://grbs.library.duke.edu/article/viewFile/1871/3501, https://www.penn.museum/sites/gordion/articles/myth-religion/the-gordian-knot/, and https://www.history.com/news/what-was-the-gordian-knot.

14. *The Fellowship of the Ring*, directed by Peter Jackson (New Line Cinema, 2001).

15. Dietrich Bonhoeffer, *Life Together*, trans. John W. Doberstein, 5th ed. (1949; repr., London: SCM Press Ltd., 2010), Kindle Edition, Loc 113.

16. Bruce Hindmarsh, "Your Job Is Not Your Savior," *Desiring God*, April 21, 2015, https://www.desiringgod.org/interviews/your-job-is-not-your-savior.

17. Tony Reinke, "Lazy Busy: Unmasking the Deadly Sin of Sloth," *Desiring God*, March 4, 2015, https://www.desiringgod.org/messages/lazy-busy.

18. C. S. Lewis, *Till We Have Faces: A Myth Retold* (New York: HarperCollins, 2017), 86.

19. Jim Kerwin, "Desire of God (a.k.a. Oh for Freedom in Worshiping God)," *Finest of the Wheat*, November 2, 2010, https://finestofthewheat.org/desire-of-god/, quoting Frederick W. Faber (1814–1863).

20. John Piper, "The Worship of the Christian Leader," *Desiring God*, November 8, 1991, https://www.desiringgod.org/messages/the-worship-of-the-christian-leader.

21. C. S. Lewis, *The Last Battle*, 1st ed. (1956; repr., New York: Collier Books, 1970), 171.

22. John Piper, *Living in the Light: Money, Sex & Power* (Charlotte, NC: The Good Book Company, 2016), 21.

23. Ibid., 149.

24. John Piper, *The Pleasures of God: Meditations on God's Delight in Being God*, 3rd ed. (1991; repr., Colorado Springs, CO: Multnomah Books, 2012), Kindle Edition. Loc. 1622.

25. Frederick Howard and Geraldine Taylor, *Hudson Taylor's Spiritual Secret* (1932; repr., Oxford, England: Benediction Classics, 2020), Kindle Edition. Loc. 1419.

26. Ibid.

27. John Piper, *A Camaraderie of Confidence: The Fruit of Unfailing Faith in the Lives of Charles Spurgeon, George Müller, and Hudson Taylor* (Wheaton, IL: Crossway, 2016), 31.

28. Ibid., 54.

29. J. R. R. Tolkien, "On Fairy Stories," in C. S. Lewis, *Essays Presented to Charles Williams* (Grand Rapids, MI: Eerdmans, 1966), 81. "Eucatastrophe" was a term first used by Tolkien to describe "the good catastrophe."

30. C. S. Lewis, *Mere Christianity* (1952; repr., New York: HarperCollins Publishers, 2017), 136.

31. John Piper, "Matthew 6:24–34, Part 3: Your Father Knows What You Need," *Desiring God*, April 30, 2015, https://www.desiringgod.org/labs/your-father-knows-what-you-need.

32. Eugene H. Peterson and Leif Peterson, *A Long Obedience in the Same Direction: Discipleship in an Instant Society* (Downers Grove, IL: IVP Books, 2019), 11.

33. John Piper, "What Is Christian Hedonism?," *Desiring God*, August 1, 2015, https://www.desiringgod.org/articles/what-is-christian-hedonism.

34. Ibid.

35. John Piper, *The Pleasures of God: Meditations on God's Delight in Being God*, 3rd ed. (1991; repr., Colorado Springs, CO: Multnomah Books, 2012), Kindle Edition. Loc. 234.

36. C. S. Lewis, *The Problem of Pain* (1940; repr., New York: HarperCollins, 2014), 150.

37. Ibid., 152.

38. Randy C. Alcorn, *Heaven* (Carol Stream, IL: Tyndale House Publishers, 2008), 165.